Knit AND Crochet WITH Beads

Knit AND Crochet WITH Beads

Lily M. Chin

INTERWEAVE PRESS
www.interweave.com

Editor: Jennifer Worick
Knitting Technical Editor: Lori Gayle
Crochet Technical Editor: Karen Manthey
Illustrations: Marjorie C. Leggitt
Photography: Joe Coca
Photo styling: Ann Swanson
Cover and interior design: Karen Schober
Production: Dean Howes and Samantha L. Thaler
Copyeditor: Stephen Beal
Proofreader and Indexer: Nancy Arndt

Interweave Press, Inc.
201 East Fourth Street
Loveland, Colorado 80537-5655 USA
www.interweave.com

Printed in China by R. R. Donnelley

Library of Congress Cataloging-in-Publication Data

Chin, Lily M.
  Bead crochet : a beadwork how-to knit and crochet with beads / Lily M. Chin.
     p. cm.
Includes index.
  ISBN 1-931499-44-6
  1. Beadwork--Patterns. 2. Knitting--Patterns. 3. Crocheting--Patterns. I. Title.
TT860.C49 2004
745.58'2--dc22
                            2003023192

10 9 8 7 6 5 4 3 2 1

Dedication

My first book I did for my mom.

The second book was for my husband.

*This, my third, goes to my sisters, Mabel and Amy.
There is nothing like a sister. Irving Berlin did a whole song
about them. They inspire and frustrate, encourage and deter.
I love my sisters dearly. Although three guys have done work
for this book, I salute the sisterhood of crafters and
handworkers everywhere.*

Contents

Acknowledgments

THERE ARE SO MANY PEOPLE I WISH TO THANK, I almost feel like I'm making a long-winded speech at the Academy Awards. First, let me thank Leigh Radford, who brought me into the project. Second, Betsy Armstrong who guided me every step of the way. Third, editors Lori Gayle, Karen Manthey, and Jennifer Worick for their keen eyes and insights. Fourth, Linda Stark for encouragement and reassurance. Fifth, Jean Campbell for being a consultant and "the enforcer." Sixth, Karen Schober and Kathryn Gamble for their artistic eye and creative input.

Of course, gratitude is expressed to yarn companies and suppliers for providing our materials. I must not forget Andrea Monfried for consultation and advice throughout three books now. Then there are the tireless stitchers: Greg Soltys (Patagonian Night Sky Scarf), Grace Judson (Ode to Pablo Neruda Socks), Cheryl Kellman (Afro-centric Vest with Wooden Beads, Raj Pillow), Bertha Falck (Trompe L'Oeil Cables, Bogus Bohus Cardigan), Thomas Jensen (Vargas Girl Pullover, Between-Stitches Floral Beaded Pockets, Cabled Tunic), Shawn Stoner (Left-Slant Floral Beaded Pockets), Barbara Hillery (Crocheted Floral Beaded Pockets), Margarete Dahlke (Ethereal Lace Tunic), Joann Moss (Homage to Haring Jacket), and Mary DuBois (Suspended in Space Stole, Plum Lines Vest).

Then there's my sister Amy who took over a lot of family duties while I labored away. Lastly, my greatest love and appreciation goes to my husband and best friend Clifford Pearson. I apologize for making him a craft-book widower!

Just like Oscar night, I hope I didn't forget anyone, and if I did, I'm sorry.

Foreword

My journey of knitting and crocheting with beads began in 1991. I'd begun to seriously learn about machine knitting and was introduced to a unique beading tool at a machine knitting conference. "Hmm," I said to myself, "why not adapt this for handknitting and crochet?"

After I'd done lots of experimenting and researching of other methods, my first published design using what were by then my many beading techniques appeared in the Fall 1993 issue of *Knitter's* magazine. In addition, my "On Design" column featured an article introducing the techniques that accompanied the design.

For machine knitters, I also did an article and design that appeared in *Machine Knit America* in May/June 1994. I followed that up with another design and article that included yet more Beaded Knitting techniques in *Knitter's* 1995 Summer issue.

It was in 1995 that I also began teaching a six-hour class for the Knitting Guild of America's national convention, held that year in St. Charles, Illinois, outside Chicago.

Subsequently, I went on to teach a class that became very popular "Bead Dazzled, Bead-Delighted, Bead-Daring, Bead Knitting!" (This book spares readers that title.) For eight years, I have taught this class at guilds, shops, and other shows such as Stitches. I offer it at least eight times a year. With twenty-five students in a class, that means I've taught my extensive techniques to more than 1,600 people!

I owe a great debt to Leigh Radford, one of these students, who worked for Interweave Press. Leigh took the class in 2002 at the Madrona Fiber Arts retreat and conference in Gig Harbor, Washington, and brought back a scouting report to the Interweave offices. Editorial Director Betsy Armstrong then approached me about doing a book on the subject.

Thus, what you have in your hands is an extremely expanded version of my already-extensive class materials. My original twelve-page handout, class samples, and completed projects have been overhauled to include more than fifteen techniques, twenty-three projects, and extensive step-by-step instructions for customizing your knitted and crocheted projects with beads of all kinds.

It is my wish that you find knitting and crocheting with beads as addictive and fun as I have for more than a decade.

Introduction

Why knit and crochet with beads?
As it is, each craft is populated with infinite
possibilities for color, pattern, and texture. Beads,
however, give knitting and crochet even more
dimension, a whole 'nuther layer, if you will.

Beads add instant texture and color. They can punctuate stitches or form their own patterns. It may seem like gilding the lily, but beads lend an even more special quality to our handknits and crochets, setting them apart from mass-produced ready-to-wear. Beads personalize a garment and announce that care and the sacred hand has touched the outcome and rendered it dear, perhaps priceless. After all, part of the reason why couture garments garner five-figure prices is their handwork or beadwork.

There are many kinds of beads, just as there are many kinds of yarns, and there are many different ways of applying beads to our knits and crochets. An infinite number of looks and effects can be achieved. The possibilities boggle the mind. To encourage individual creativity, I have devoted a special section for readers who wish to design their own creations.

Technically speaking, the term "bead knitting" refers to a fabric composed of all beads where each stitch has a bead knitted on (see Chapter 1). "Beaded knitting" refers to knits embellished here and there with beads. I've taken this distinction from *Mary Thomas' Knitting Book* (see Sources and Further Reading, page 148).

Generally speaking, there are three broad ways to apply beads to knitted and crocheted pieces.

1. Integrated into the Fabric/Knitted or Crocheted In. Beads are prestrung on the yarn to become an integral part of the fabric, or unstrung beads are hoisted on whole stitches to become an integral part of the fabric.

2. A separate strand of yarn with beads on it is either woven between stitches or is knitted/crocheted along with the yarn; the beads are a semi-integral part of the fabric.

3. Beads are sewn or embroidered onto fabric after it is knitted or crocheted. Here beads are embellishment and are not integral to the fabric.

The first method involves the most preplanning and meticulous care. The second method involves some preplanning, and the third is the most spontaneous and does not require much preplanning.

The method(s) you choose will no doubt be determined by the effort you wish to invest, the nature of the particular project, and the effect of each method. I give you all the options so you can determine which you prefer. You may even combine methods in any particular piece!

If you're anything like me, the ideas will come fast and furious. There may be more ideas than a lifetime can allow! Ah, the possibilities. . . .

Techniques AND Projects

CHAPTER I

Preparation
The Beads

Beads can be glamorous or primitive, glitzy or rustic, delicate or bold. They come in a wide selection of materials whose properties differ. Wood beads are usually matte and lightweight (though they are often coated with a shiny varnish); they're durable, delicate, or in-between. Plastic is usually shiny, lightweight, and versatile, with finishes that resemble metal or glass or other natural materials. Metal is typically shiny and heavy and quite durable. Glass is often shiny, heavy, and delicate. Then there are the miscellaneous types of beads: shell, clay, semiprecious stones, porcelain, synthetics (like Fimo clay), bone, and more.

Various bead types

Various yarn types

Stringing beads

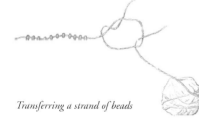

Transferring a strand of beads

The Big "Eye" needle

The materials normally define the look you're trying to achieve. Wood and bone tend to be rustic. Glass and some metals are generally dressier.

For knitting or crocheting with beads, the hole must be big enough to accommodate the yarn. Actually, the hole must accommodate two strands of yarn, at least in the stringing process (see illustration at left). The bead itself should be large enough to stand out and not get imbedded or buried and lost in the stitches. However, too heavy or too large a bead distorts and/or pulls the knitted or crocheted fabric. The garment gets weighty and/or bulky.

Ideally, yarn matches bead in three respects:
• Size
• Washability/wearability
• Mood or feel

Remember—plastics can melt, metals can tarnish, shells can chip, yarns can stretch, fibers can fray. When in doubt, test the swatch out!

Prestringing

To prestring beads, I especially like the Big "Eye" beading needle, one formed by two lengths of thin, flexible wire joined at both ends. Using the thumbnail, separate the center to open up the needle (much like a archer's bow). Insert yarn to thread.

Ingenious, yes? Don't lose this needle (you can keep bit of yarn in the eye for easy identification). I usually bring my intended project yarn threaded on the needle to a bead store to make sure the yarn can fit through the bead holes. Conversely, I bring beads and the needle into a yarn shop to find a yarn that will go through the bead hole. Place beads in a shallow dish or small bowl to prevent loss and restrict rolling.

Of course, there are also thin beading needles available, very much like regular sewing needles, but much finer and usually longer. In a pinch, you can fashion a makeshift beading needle from piano wire or nylon floss folded in half. Place the yarn at the looped center, then place both open ends through the beads. Dental floss threaders are also perfect for threading beads and their ends are already fused together.

Some beads come on strands. Tie a simple knot of the thread the beads are on around the yarn for stringing, then slide the beads over.

Because beads may be pushed along the strand of yarn as you work until you need them, the yarn should be sturdy enough for this sort of abrasion, which will depend on the number of beads. The yarn should also be smooth. There are ways around these strictures, however, as proven by the cashmere Vargas Girl Pullover and Afro-centric Vest with Wooden Beads. The other exceptions are those methods that do not require prestringing beads on yarn.

When you're working with prestrung beads, shove them down the yarn in small batches, as many as it takes to move down easily. You will need to reel off some slack in your yarn for actual knitting or crocheting, but leave a few beads behind every few inches or so. That way, they are readily available when needed. I have been known to leave a trail of yarn around my living-room floor to knit or crochet with. To prevent tangling, do not overlap reelings. I do a series of U-turns away from me. Of course, it helps if you have floor space that doesn't get a lot of foot traffic. I've actually entertained the idea of hanging the beaded skein out of my fifth-floor apartment window and letting it dangle!

About two-thirds to three-quarters of the beads required may be strung first, with the remaining one-third to one-quarter added from the end of the skein instead. This method is for single-color and/or types of beads that do not require any particular order in the stringing.

Trailing yarns

Bead Knitting vs Beaded Knitting

As I outline in the introduction, there is a distinction between the terms "Bead Knitting" and "Beaded Knitting."

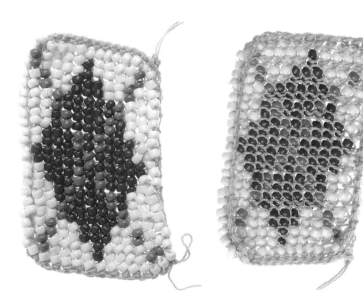

Left: Front of bead knitted argyle swatch

Right: Back of bead knitted argyle swatch

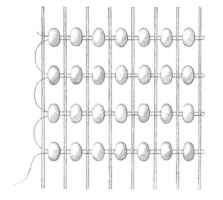

Loom-beaded fabric

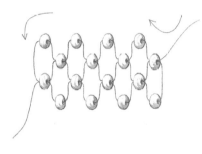

Peyote-stitch fabric

Bead knitted heart swatch, slanting left

Bead Knitting refers to a fabric primarily made up of beads. No yarn is visible, except on the back of the fabric.

View the front of the argyle swatch on page 8. Notice how very little of the yellow thread is seen. A bead is knitted through each and every stitch. It is not until you view the back of this swatch that you see how the yellow, knitted backing keeps each bead suspended on the fabric.

Beaded Knitting refers to any other type of knitting where beads are employed to embellish the fabric. What is seen here is primarily the knitted fabric, with beads scattered on top. The vast majority of knitting which employs beads will be of the Beaded Knitting variety. Bead Knitting is a rather specialized technique that requires tremendous skill, patience, and fortitude. Thus, most of this book is devoted to Beaded Knitting, with Bead Knitting covered only in Chapter 5.

While Bead Knitting most resembles the type of fabric made in loom beading, or even a peyote fabric, there are great differences. In loom beading, to create multicolored patterns, one threads up the beads in an exact order with every pass of the weft or with every horizontal row. In peyote stitch, the beads are offset and horizontal. In Bead Knitting, the order of the beads must be predetermined far in advance for a long stretch of knitting.

Also, in needle-beading, the beads lie on a horizontal thread. In Bead Knitting, the thread that holds the bead gets knitted. The bead therefore follows the looped and convoluted path of the thread and ends up sitting at an angle, very much like the earth on its axis. In turn, this angle makes the final fabric bias. Thus asymmetrically shaped beads with a clear direction, such as a heart (see left), don't do well in Bead Knitting.

Since Bead Knitting was at its height during the Victorian era, it was used primarily to simulate needlepoint. Unfortunately, just as in needlepoint, the piece torques, both in pattern and overall shape.

For further discussion and investigation of knitting and crocheting using beads, please refer to the specific techniques detailed in the chapters that follow.

CHAPTER 2

Beaded Knitting:
Prestrung, between Stitches

Patagonian Night Sky Scarf,
Ode to Pablo Neruda Socks,
Harry Winston Has Nothing on Me Necklace,
Trompe L'Oeil Cables

This first method presented is one of the easiest. To begin, prestring the yarn with beads as per Chapter 1 (see page 7). As you knit, push the bead up to the knitting so it lies on the strand of yarn between two stitches. The bead lies on its side and is supported by the strand of yarn between the stitches. Thus, I recommend a fairly firm gauge.

Note: I use the abbreviation BUB often. It stands for Bring Up Bead. That is, snuggle up the bead near the needle.

In order for the bead to show on the public side of the work, purls must be employed. In stockinette stitch (knit on the right side, purl on the wrong side), you may flank the place where you want a bead to appear with purls. Thus, on a right side, knit up to within a stitch of where you want a bead placed, purl the next stitch, BUB, purl the stitch after the bead, then resume knitting. The swatch at right illustrates this process.

In garter stitch, you can place a bead only on a ridge row (knit on wrong side). Thus, beads appear only every other row.

In seed stitch, the bead has a 50-percent chance of falling to the wrong side and thus the use of seed stitch in beading is only semieffective.

Ribbing obscures the beads totally, though the bead still has a 50-percent chance of falling to the right or wrong side.

Beaded knitting in ribbing

Beaded knitting in seed stitch

Beaded knitting in stockinette stitch

Beaded knitting in garter stitch

Reverse stockinette stitch (purl on right side, knit on wrong side) presents the most options.

An interesting effect occurs when the beads are behind the fabric of stockinette stitch and just peek through between the stitches. The use of larger beads and the vertical stacking help make this effect more dramatic.

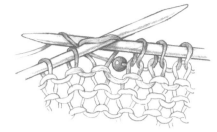

Beaded knitting on the knit side

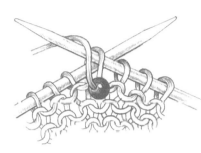

Beaded knitting on the purl side

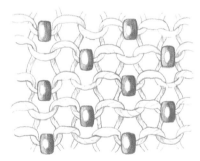

Beaded knitting in reverse stockinette stitch

A vertical line of beading in stockinette stitch

Patagonian Night Sky Scarf

While a full shawl in allover beadwork may prove too heavy, a shoulder scarf fills the bill. This elegant cover-up can warm chilly shoulders when it's worn with a strapless evening dress. Or choose a less dressy yarn like the Jaeger Cashmina (used in the Vargas Girl Pullover) with a matte bead for a daytime look you can wear over a blouse.

Finished Size
About 18" (45.5 cm) high from top edge to bottom of point, and 42" (106.5 cm) wide across top edge.

Materials
- Yarn: Rowan Lurex Shimmer (80% viscose, 20% polyester; 104 yd [95 m]/25 g): #339 midnight, 7 skeins. Yarn distributed in U.S. by Rowan/Westminster Fibers.

- Beads: Size 10mm or size 6 seed beads: about 2,700. Shown in clear silver-lined, from Rowan/Westminster Fibers.

- Needles: Size 3 (3.25 mm): circular. Adjust needle size if necessary to obtain the correct gauge.

- Notions: Bead-stringing needle; tapestry needle; stitch markers (optional).

Gauge
26 sts and 60 rows (30 garter ridges) = 4" (10 cm) in garter st (knit all sts every row).

Yarn around needle with bead at beginning of row

Special Notes
Prestring beads on yarn before working, about 350–400 beads per skein.

Special Abbreviations
BUB: Bring Up Bead, snuggle the bead up close to the needle. Each bead will lie on the yarn strand between two stitches when you are knitting a row on the WS (to form a garter ridge). Beads in the body and last row of the scarf will lie on the RS of the scarf fabric; beads added at the beginning of rows will lie along the diagonal edges of the scarf.

Yon: Yarn around needle, or a yarnover produced in a knitwise fashion.

Instructions
CO 2 sts. Work Rows 1–7 of chart, adding a bead at the beg of each row starting with Row 2. Rows 1–7 are written out in words as follows:

Row 1: (RS) K2.
Row 2: (WS) BUB, k2.
Row 3: BUB, yon, k2—3 sts.
Row 4: BUB, yon, k3—4 sts.
Row 5: BUB, yon, k4—5 sts.
Row 6: BUB, yon, k5—6 sts.

Row 7: BUB, yon, k6—7 sts.

From here on, every row will be worked as BUB, yon, work in pattern to end. There will be a bead at the beginning of every row, each row will add 1 more st, and after you complete each row the number of sts should equal the row number.

Beginning with Row 8, add beads in the body of the scarf as shown on chart. Rows 8–14 are written out in words as follows:

Row 8: (WS) BUB, yon, k3, BUB, k4—8 sts.

Row 9 and all RS rows: BUB, yon, knit to end—1 st increased.

Row 10: BUB, yon, k3, BUB, k2, BUB, k4—10 sts.

Row 12: BUB, yon, k5, BUB, k6—12 sts.

Row 14: BUB, yon, knit to end—14 sts.

Work Rows 15–30 from chart—30 sts. Repeat Rows 15–30 fifteen more times, continuing to add a bead at the beginning of each row as established; you may find it helpful to place markers between each pattern repeat—270 sts; 270 rows completed. Work a RS row—271 sts; 271 rows completed. On the next row (WS) BO with beads as follows: [K1, p1] in same st to inc 1, pass first st over second st to BO 1, *BUB, [k1, pass first st over second st to BO 1] twice; rep from * across. Weave in ends.

☐ knit on RS	⚫•⚫ k1, BUB, k1 on WS
• knit on WS	☐ pattern repeat
⚪ yon	

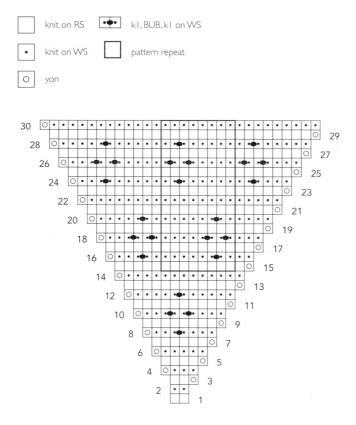

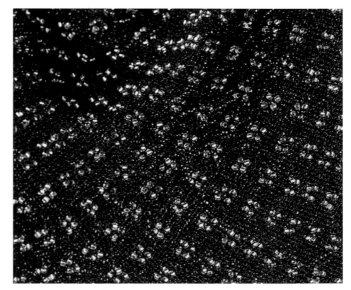

Ode to Pablo Neruda Socks

The beads here will knock your socks off! Well, not quite. They *will* make knockout socks, however. The stacked diagonal lines help hold the sock up, even though the socks look just as good slouched. Notice the mirror-image diagonals. Wear the socks on either foot, then switch them around for fun.

Finished Size

To fit U.S. shoe sizes child's 10–12 (woman's 5–6, woman's 7–8, woman's 9–10 or man's 8–9, man's 10–11).

Finished foot circumference 5¼ (6½, 7¾, 9, 10½)" (13.5 [16.5, 19.5, 23, 26.5] cm)

Finished foot length: 6½ (8¼, 9, 10, 10¾)" (16.5 [21, 23, 25.5, 27.5] cm)

Socks shown in U.S. shoe size woman's 5–6.

Materials

- Yarn: Brown Sheep Wildfoote (75% washable wool, 25% nylon; 215 yd [196 m]/50 g): #SY19 temple turquoise, 1 (2, 2, 2, 2) skeins.

- Beads: Size 6 seed beads, about 575 (700, 850, 975, 1,125), color, supplier, and style number not available.

- Needles: Size 1 (2.5 mm): set of 4 double-pointed (dpn). Adjust needle size if necessary to obtain the correct gauge.

- Notions: Bead-stringing needle; tapestry needle.

Gauge

37 sts and 48 rows = 4" (10 cm) in diagonal pattern stitch worked in the round (rnd) without beads.

Special Notes

Prestring beads on yarn before working, about 240 (300, 360, 420, 480) beads per sock.

Special Abbreviations

BUB: Bring Up Bead, snuggle the bead up close to the needle. Beads will lie on the RS on the yarn strand between two purl sts.

First Sock

CO 48 (60, 72, 84, 96) sts. Arrange on 3 dpns so that there are 16 (20, 24, 28, 32) sts on each needle (ndl). Work 12 rnds of first sock cuff pattern from chart, or written out in words as follows:

Rnd 1: *K2, p1, BUB, p1, k2; rep from * around.
Rnd 2: *P1, k1, p1; rep from * around.
Rnd 3: *K1, p1, BUB, p1, k3; rep from * around.
Rnd 4: *K1, p2; rep from * around.
Rnd 5: *P1, BUB, p1, k4; rep from * around.
Rnd 6: *P2, k1; rep from * around.
Rnd 7: *BUB, p1, k4, p1; rep from * around.
Rnd 8: Rep Rnd 2.
Rnd 9: *K4, p1, BUB, p1; rep from * around.
Rnd 10: Rep Rnd 4.
Rnd 11: *K3, p1, BUB, p1, k1; rep from * around.
Rnd 12: Rep Rnd 6.

Change to first sock diagonal pattern and work Rnds 1–12 from chart, or written out in words as follows:

Rnd 1: *K2, p1, BUB, p1, k2; rep from * around.

Rnd 2: *K2, p2, k2; rep from * around.

Rnd 3: *K1, p1, BUB, p1, k3; rep from * around.

Rnd 4: *K1, p2, k3; rep from * around.

Rnd 5: *P1, BUB, p1, k4; rep from * around.

Rnd 6: *P2, k4; rep from * around.

Rnd 7: *BUB, p1, k4, p1; rep from * around.

Rnd 8: *P1, k4, p1; rep from * around.

Rnd 9: *K4, p1, BUB, p1; rep from * around.

Rnd 10: *K4, p2; rep from * around.

Rnd 11: *K3, p1, BUB, p1, k1; rep from * around.

Rnd 12: *K3, p2, k1; rep from * around.

Rep Rnds 1–12, until piece measures 6 (6½, 6½, 7, 7)" (15 [16.5, 16.5, 18, 18] cm) or desired length to beginning of heel, roughly even with the center of the ankle bone. Note which rnd you end with so you can resume the pattern in the right place for the foot after the heel is completed.

Short Row Heel

Arrange the stitches so that there are 24 (30, 36, 42, 48) sts on first ndl, 12 (15, 18, 21, 24) sts on second ndl, and 12 (15, 18, 21, 24) sts on third ndl. The heel is worked back and forth on the sts of the first ndl. Work the heel without beads in St st (knit on RS, purl on WS). All slipped (sl) sts are slipped as if to purl.

First Half of Heel

Row 1: Knit to the last st of first ndl. With yarn in back (wyib), sl the last st to the right ndl. Turn.

Row 2: Sl first st wyib. Bring yarn to the front between the ndls; the yarn is now fully wrapped around the sl st. Purl to the last st. With yarn in front (wyif), sl last st. Turn.

Row 3: Sl first st wyif. Bring yarn to the back between the ndls; the yarn is now fully wrapped around the sl st—1 st wrapped at each end of ndl, 22 (28, 34, 40, 46) sts between the wrapped sts. Knit to 1 st before the previously wrapped st, sl next st wyib, bring yarn to front, and turn.

Row 4: Sl next st wyib. Bring yarn to the front; yarn is now fully wrapped around the sl st. Purl to 1 st before previously wrapped st. Sl the next st wyif, bring yarn to the back between the ndls, and turn.

Row 5: Sl next st wyif. Bring yarn to the back; yarn is now fully wrapped around the sl st. Knit to 1 st before previously wrapped st. Sl next st wyib, bring yarn to front, and turn.

Rep Rows 4 and 5 a total of 5 (7, 9, 11, 13) more times, then work Row 4 once more, ending with a row that has 8 (10, 12, 14, 16) sts purled between the wrapped sts. Turn the work, sl next st wyif. There

| | knit | | • | purl | | •●• | p1, BUB, p1 |

First Sock Cuff

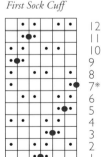

*Work Rnd 7 as *BUB, p1, k4, p1; rep from * around.

First Sock Diagonal Pattern

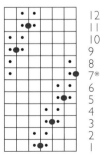

*Work Rnd 7 as *BUB, p1, k4, p1; rep from * around.

should be 8 (10, 12, 14, 16) wrapped sts at each end of ndl.

Second Half of Heel

Row 1: K8 (10, 12, 14, 16) sts to arrive at first wrapped st. *Insert right ndl into both the wrapped st and its wrap, inserting the ndl into front of wrap from bottom to top as if to knit. Knit both the st and its wrap together (tog); this may be a little tricky, but do your best to wriggle the new loop through. Rep from * to the end of the ndl. Turn.

Row 2: Sl the first st, purl to the first wrapped st. *With tip of right needle, pick up the wrap from behind the work and lift it onto the left needle. Purl both the st and its wrap tog. Rep from * to end of ndl. Turn.

Row 3: Slip the first st, k15 (19, 23, 27, 31), sl next st wyib, bring yarn to front, return sl st to left ndl, turn.

Row 4: P8 (10, 12, 14, 16), sl next st wyif, bring yarn to back, return sl st to left ndl, turn.

Row 5: Knit to wrapped st, knit st and its wrap tog as before, sl next st wyib, bring yarn to front, return sl st to left ndl, turn.

Row 6: Purl to wrapped st, purl the st and its wrap tog as before, sl the next st wyif, bring yarn to back, return sl st to left ndl, turn.

Rep Rows 5 and 6 until all sts on heel ndl have been worked, ending with a purl row.

Foot

Place marker to indicate new beg of rnd—48 (60, 72, 84, 96) sts. The first and second ndls with 12 (15, 18, 21, 24) sts each are the instep, and the third ndl with 24 (30, 36, 42, 48) sts from working the heel is the underside of the foot. Resume first sock diagonal pattern where you left off, and work pattern around on all sts, without beads, until foot measures 5¼ (6¾, 7, 7¾, 8¼)" (13.5 [17, 18, 19.5, 21] cm) from back of heel, or about 1¼ (1½, 2, 2¼, 2½)" (3.2 [3.8, 5, 5.5, 6.5] cm) less than desired length. Try on sock; it should reach just about to the base of the little toe. Adjust length here, if necessary.

Toe

Rnd 1: (Decrease Rnd) On first ndl k1, ssk, knit to end; on second ndl knit to last 3 sts, k2tog, k1; on third ndl k1, ssk, knit to last 3 sts, k2tog, k1.

Rnd 2: Knit all sts.

Rep Rnds 1 and 2 until 16 (20, 24, 28, 32) sts remain, ending with Rnd 1. Sl the sts for the instep onto a single needle—8 (10, 12, 14, 16) sts each on 2 ndls. Cut yarn, leaving a 16" (40.5 cm) tail. Thread tail on tapestry needle and graft the end of the toe closed.

Second Sock

Prestring more beads on yarn, if necessary.

CO 48 (60, 72, 84, 96) sts. Arrange on 3 dpns so that there are 16 (20, 24, 28, 32) sts on each ndl. Work 12 rnds of second sock cuff pattern from chart, or written out in words as follows:

Rnd 1: *K2, p1, BUB, p1, k2; rep from * around.

Rnd 2: *P1, k1, p1; rep from * around.

Rnd 3: *K3, p1, BUB, p1, k1; rep from * around.

Rnd 4: *P2, k1; rep from * around.

Rnd 5: *K4, p1, BUB, p1; rep from * around.

Rnd 6: *K1, p2; rep from * around.

Rnd 7: *P1, k4, p1, BUB; rep from * around.

Rnd 8: Rep Rnd 2.

Rnd 9: *P1, BUB, p1, k4; rep from * around.

Rnd 10: Rep Rnd 4.

Rnd 11: *K1, p1, BUB, p1, k3; rep from * around.

Rnd 12: Rep Rnd 6.

Change to second sock diagonal pattern and work Rnds 1–12 from chart, or written out in words as follows:

Rnd 1: *K2, p1, BUB, p1, k2; rep from * around.

Rnd 2: *K2, p2, k2; rep from * around.

Rnd 3: *K3, p1, BUB, p1, k1; rep from * around.

Rnd 4: *K3, p2, k1; rep from * around.

Rnd 5: *K4, p1, BUB, p1; rep from * around.

Rnd 6: *K4, p2; rep from * around.

Rnd 7: *P1, k4, p1, BUB; rep from * around.

Rnd 8: *P1, k4, p1; rep from * around.

Rnd 9: *P1, BUB, p1, k4; rep from * around.

Rnd 10: *P2, k4; rep from * around.

Rnd 11: *K1, p1, BUB, p1, k3; rep from * around.

Rnd 12: *K1, p2, k3; rep from * around.

Rep Rnds 1–12, until piece measures 6 (6½, 6½, 7, 7)" (15 [16.5, 16.5, 18, 18] cm) or desired length to beginning of heel, roughly even with the center of the ankle bone. Note which rnd you end with so you can resume the pattern in the right place for the foot after the heel is completed.

Short Row Heel, Foot, and Toe

Work as for first sock, substituting second sock diagonal pattern for foot.

Finishing

Weave in ends. Block lightly, if desired.

knit   purl   p1, BUB, p1

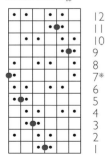

Second Sock Cuff

*Work Rnd 7 as *p1, k4, p1, BUB; rep from * around.

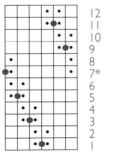

Second Sock Diagonal Pattern

*Work Rnd 7 as *p1, k4, p1, BUB; rep from * around.

Harry Winston Has Nothing on Me Necklace

Pairing slinky silk with matching copper beads gives this piece of jewelry a fancy edge. Create a sportier version by using cotton or linen with matte or wood beads, perhaps in a contrasting color. This piece sits lower on the neck than a choker and feels just like a necklace, right down to the clasp closure. The lace pattern curves in a natural arc.

Finished Size
About 17" (43 cm) long, not including clasp.

Materials
- Yarn: Gudebrod Silk Thread Size E (100% silk; 200 yd [183 m]/spool): #12–1127BS brown, 1 spool.

- Beads: Size 12 glass seed beads: about 450. Shown in #601 copper from Beads World.

- Needles: Size 000 (1.5 mm): straight or double-pointed. Adjust needle size if necessary to obtain the correct gauge.

- Notions: Bead-stringing needle; tapestry needle; gold metal clasp; sharp-pointed sewing needle and matching thread (to attach clasp).

Gauge
11 sts and 16 row = 1" (2.5 cm) in beaded pattern.

Special Notes
Prestring beads on yarn before working.

Special Abbreviations
BUB: Bring Up Bead, snuggle bead up close to the needle.

Instructions
CO 8 sts. Work in pattern from chart; Rows 1–8 are written out in words as follows:

Row 1: (WS) K1, BUB, k2, yo, k2tog, yo twice, k2tog, BUB, k1—9 sts.

Row 2: (RS) K2, drop one of the next 2 yo's; work k1, p1 in remaining yo; k2, yo, k2tog, k1.

Row 3: K1, BUB, k2, yo, k2tog, BUB, k1, yo twice, k2 tog, BUB, k1—10 sts.

Row 4: K2, drop one of the next 2 yo's; work k1, p1 in remaining yo; k3, yo, k2tog, k1.

Row 5: K1, BUB, k2, yo, k2tog, k1, BUB, k1, yo twice, k2 tog, BUB, k1—11 sts.

Row 6: K2, drop one of the next 2 yo's; work k1, p1 in remaining yo; k4, yo, k2tog, k1.

Row 7: K1, BUB, k2, yo, k2tog, k2, BUB, k3, BUB, k1.

Row 8: BO 3 sts (1 st on right needle), k4 (5 sts on right needle), yo, k2tog, k1—8 sts.

Repeat Rows 1–8 for pattern until piece measures 17" (43 cm) or desired length, and end having just completed Row 8 of patt. BO all sts.

Finishing
Block piece if desired. Weave in ends. Sew ½ of clasp to each end.

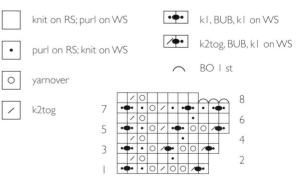

	knit on RS; purl on WS		k1, BUB, k1 on WS
•	purl on RS; knit on WS		k2tog, BUB, k1 on WS
O	yarnover		BO 1 st
╱	k2tog		

Trompe L'Oeil Cables

The bead patterning in this tank top creates the illusion of cables. The French call it *trompe l'oeil*, or "tricking the eye." The pattern requires no real turning of stitches, but it does turn heads. Sleeves may be added raglan-style to create a full sweater since this tank has halter-type shaping. Dress it up by using a metallic yarn like Skacel's Karat (this knits to the same gauge as the yarn used here). Add glitzier beads for painting the town.

Finished Size

35 (37½, 40½, 44, 46½)" (89 [95, 103, 112, 118] cm) bust/chest circumference. Tank top shown measures 37½" (95 cm). This garment is intended to be close-fitting with minimal ease.

Materials

- Yarn: Skacel Polo (60% cotton, 40% microfiber; 153 yd [140 m]/50 g): #84 toast, 5 (6, 7, 8, 9) skeins.

- Beads: Size 6 seed beads: about 2,750 (2,800, 2,850, 2,900, 2,950). Shown in #F736, variegated rose and fuchsia, from Toho Shoji.

- Needles: Tank—Size 6 (4 mm): straight and 16" (40-cm) circular (cir). Ribbing—Size 4 (3.5 mm): straight and 16" (40-cm) cir, or 2 sizes smaller than main needles. Adjust needle size if necessary to obtain the correct gauge.

- Notions: Bead-stringing needle; stitch markers, stitch holders, tapestry needle.

Gauge

20 sts and 28 rows = 4" (10 cm) in St st.

Special Notes

Prestring beads on yarn before working, about 450 beads per skein; front and back each take about half the beads. If necessary, add more beads from the end of the skein.

For the neckband worked in the round (rnd), work all rows of the chart as RS rnds.

Special Abbreviations

BUB: Bring Up Bead, snuggle the bead up close to the needle. Beads will lie on the RS on the yarn strand between two purl sts.

Back

With smaller straight needles, CO 88 (94, 102, 110, 116) sts. Work Rows 1 and 2 of ribbing as follows:

Row 1: (RS) K1 (4, 8, 12, 15), p1, BUB, p1, [k2, p1, BUB, p2, BUB, p1] twice, [k2, p1, BUB, p1] 14 times, [k2, p1, BUB, p2, BUB, p1] twice, k2, p1, BUB, p1, end k1 (4, 8, 12, 15).

Row 2: (WS) Purl across.

Rep Rows 1 and 2 until ribbing measures 3" (7.5 cm); end having just completed a WS row.

Change to larger straight needles. Set up patt from chart as follows: Work 1 (4, 8 12, 15) sts in St st, work center 86 sts according to Row 1 of chart, work 1 (4, 8, 12, 15) sts in St st. Keeping sts at each side of chart in St st, work Rows 2–32 of chart once, then rep Rows 1–32 of chart until piece measures 12" (30.5 cm) from beg; end having just completed a WS row.

Shape armholes: Cont in patt from chart, BO 4 (5, 6, 7, 8) sts at the beg of the next 2 rows—80 (84, 90, 96, 100) sts rem. On the next RS row, dec 1 st at each end of row as follows: K1, ssk, work in patt to last 3 sts, k2tog, k1—2 sts decreased. Work 1 WS row. Rep the last 2 rows 9 (9, 12, 14, 14) more times, then work the decrease row every fourth row 3 (4, 3, 3, 4) times, then work the decrease row every sixth row once—52 (54, 56, 58, 60) sts rem. Work even until armholes measure 6½ (7, 7½, 8, 8½)" (16.5 [18, 19, 20.5, 21.5] cm); end having just completed a WS row.

Shape shoulders: Cont in patt from chart, BO 2 sts at the beg of the next 2 rows—48 (50, 52, 54, 56) sts. Place sts on holder. Note which row you end with so you can resume the pattern in the right place for the neckband later.

Front

Work same as the back.

Finishing

Weave in ends. Block pieces to measurements. Sew shoulder seams. Sew side seams.

Neckband

Return sts from holder to larger cir needle, and join yarn at left shoulder for working in the rnd. Cont in patt, work across 48 (50, 52, 54, 56) sts of front, place marker (pm), work across 48 (50, 52, 54, 56) sts of back, pm for

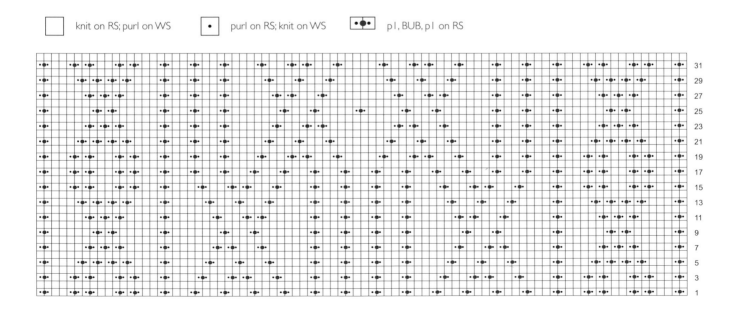

end of rnd—96 (100, 104, 108, 112) sts. Cont in patt from chart, working in the rnd with the RS of piece facing you at all times. Next rnd: Cont in patt from chart, *work to 1 st before marker (m), sl 1 st to right needle, temporarily remove m, return sl st to left ndl, k2tog (last st of one piece and first of the other), replace m; rep from * once more—94 (98, 102, 106, 110) sts. Cont in patt from chart until neckband measures 3" (7.5 cm). BO all sts loosely as if to knit, without beads.

Armhole Bands

Prestring 45 (48, 50, 53, 55) beads on yarn. With RS facing and smaller cir needle, beg at the side seam, pick up and knit 90 (96, 100, 106, 110) sts evenly spaced around armhole. Pm to indicate beg of rnd. Work in the rnd with the RS of piece facing you at all times. Next rnd: *P1, BUB, p1, rep from * around. On the following rnd, BO all sts loosely as if to knit, without beads. Repeat for other armhole.

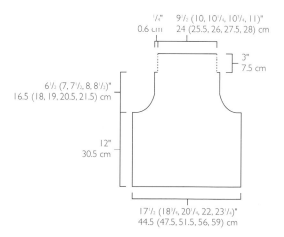

Beaded Knitting:
Prestrung, atop Slip Stitches
Afro-centric Vest with Wooden Beads

This method employs slipped stitches, with the yarn to the right side of the work. Each bead is pushed up to the knitting, where it lies on the strand of yarn as a float atop the slipped stitch.

Bead sits on top of slip stitch in front

The stitch that the bead sits on top of is not knitted but slipped instead. Always slip as if to purl. The bead sits on top of the unknitted stitch on the floated strand of yarn. Thus, on the wrong side of stockinette stitch (or the purl side), bring the yarn to the back when a bead is desired, slip the stitch, bring the bead up to the needle and keep it to the back of the work (or the right side), then bring the yarn to the front again to purl. On the right side of stockinette stitch (or the knit side), bring the yarn to the front when a bead is desired, slip the stitch, bring the bead up to the needle and keep it to the front of the work (or the right side), then bring the yarn to the back again to knit. This method may be employed in any stitch pattern, as long as the yarn is to the right side of the slip stitch(es).

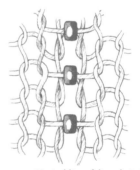

Vertical line of slipped stitches

If a bead is particularly long, more than one stitch may be slipped. I suggest no more than five stitches be slipped consecutively; too long a float, as in stranded color-work, can catch on fingers, rings, and the like. This method is also not very secure. I advise against heavy or weighty beads since the only thing holding the bead up is that floated strand of yarn. For this reason, springier or more elastic yarns can be used with great results. An inelastic yarn may prove too limp to hold the bead, unless a firm gauge is employed. The advantage to this method, however, is that the bead stands out. The fabric from behind forces the bead forward.

Note: You can't constantly slip/not-knit the same stitch over and over again. Thus, if you desire a vertical "stacking" of beads, slip every other row.

Notice how, in both methods presented so far, the bead is horizontal or lying on its side and is held in place by a single strand of yarn. If you're not careful, your crescent moon may become a frown or that figurine you thought would look good rendered in beads will be lying down on the job!

Heart beads both between-stitches and slipped

Afro-centric Vest with Wooden Beads

Displaying a decidedly ethnic feel, this vest can be worn by itself as a tank top or camisole. For warmer climes, try substituting Louet Sales Euroflax Linen, sportweight. The unusual construction results in beads lying in different directions, horizontally in the center panels and vertically at the side panels. Because the type and shape of beads alternate, take special care in the stringing order (it's clearly spelled out in the directions).

Finished Size

36 (40, 44, 48)" (91.5 [101.5, 112, 122] cm) bust/chest circumference. Vest shown measures 40" (101.5 cm).

Materials

- Yarn: Gems Merino Opal (100% Merino superwash wool; 225 yd [206 m]/100 g): #23 tobacco, 4 (5, 5, 6, 6) skeins. Yarn distributed in North America by Louet Sales.

- Beads: 4mm round wooden beads: about 1,250 (1,300, 1,350, 1,450). Shown in #1076NB Brown. 10mm × 6mm long melon-shaped wooden beads: about 400 (400, 475, 550). Shown in #1094NB Brown. All beads from Fire Mountain Gems.

- Needles: Vest—Size 6 (4 mm): straight. Neck and Armhole Finishing—Size 6 (4 mm): 16" (40-cm) circular (cir). Adjust needle size if necessary to obtain the correct gauge.

- Notions: Bead-stringing needle; extra set of needles in same size or smaller for three-needle bind-off; tapestry needle; crochet hook size E4 (3.5 mm).

Gauge

21 sts and 45 rows = 4" (10 cm) in center back panel pattern; 21 sts and 49 rows = 4" (10 cm) in center front panel pattern; and 21 sts and 42 rows = 4" (10 cm) in side panel pattern.

Special Notes

Center back and front panels are worked first, each from the bottom up. Stitches are picked up for the side panels from each side of the center front panel. The side panels are worked outward around to the back and joined to the center back panel.

Prestring beads on yarn before working, stringing them in the reverse sequence in which they will be used. In other words, the last bead strung on the yarn will be the first bead used in the pattern.

Work with two separate strands of yarn, one with beads strung on it, and one without beads, the way you would when you're making a garment with stripes in two colors. When you get to a beading row (WS), change to the strand with beads, work the next 2 rows, then switch back to the strand without beads.

When there is a long interval without beads, carry the beaded strand along the selvedge, "catching" the unused strand every few rows by twisting the two strands together to prevent a long float on the sides (see illustration at right).

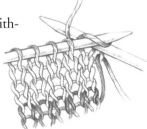

Catching the yarn not in use at the edge

Always slip the first stitch of every row as if to purl with the yarn in front of the work (wyif). The slipped selvedge stitches will make it easy to pick up stitches when you're joining and finishing the garment pieces.

Each long bead is backed by 3 slipped stitches; each round bead is backed by 1 slipped stitch.

Special Abbreviations

BUB: Bring Up Bead, snuggle the bead up close to the needle. Beads will lie on the RS on the yarn strand in front of the slipped stitches.

BUBL: Bring up long bead.

BUBR: Bring up round bead.

Center Back Panel

Prestring one strand with 408 (425, 442, 459) round beads. With separate unbeaded strand, CO 39 sts and knit 2 rows, slipping the first st of each row with yarn in front (wyif). Work in pattern from center back panel chart; Rows 1–8 are written out in words as follows:

Row 1: (WS) With unbeaded strand, sl 1 st wyif, knit to end.

Row 2: (RS) Rep Row 1.

Row 3: (WS) With unbeaded strand, sl 1 st wyif, k1, *sl 1 st with yarn in back (wyib; float will be on the RS of

work), bring yarn to front and p1; rep from * to last 3 sts, sl 1 st wyib, k2.

Rows 4–6: Rep Row 1.

Row 7: (bead row, WS) With beaded strand, sl 1 st wyif, k1, *p1, sl 1 st wyib, BUBR; rep from * to last 3 sts, p1, k2.

Row 8: With beaded strand, sl 1 st wyif, knit to end, but do not bring up any beads.

Repeat Rows 1–8 from chart or as above, 23 (24, 25, 26) more times, then work the first 6 (4, 2, 0) rows of the pattern once more—198 (204, 210, 216) pattern rows; 24 (25, 26, 27) bead rows. Knit 4 rows, slipping the first st of each row wyif—piece measures about 18 (18½, 19, 19½)" (45.5 [47, 48.5, 49.5] cm) from beg. BO as if to knit on next WS row.

Center Front Panel

Prestring one strand with 520 (528, 548, 560) round and 130 (135, 140, 140) long beads in the following order: [1 long bead, 4 round beads, 3 long beads, 4 round beads, 1 long bead] 0 (1, 1, 0) time(s), then [12 round beads, 1 long bead, 4 round beads, 3 long beads, 4 round beads, 1 long bead] 26 (26, 27, 28) times. With separate unbeaded strand, CO 39 sts and knit 2 rows, slipping the first st of each row with yarn in front (wyif). Work in pattern from center front panel chart; Rows 1–8 are written out in words as follows:

Row 1: (WS) With unbeaded strand, sl 1 st wyif, knit to end.

	knit on RS; purl on WS		sl 1 wyib, BUBR on WS
•	purl on RS; knit on WS		sl 3 wyib, BUBL on WS
ⱶ	sl 1 wyib on WS; sl 1 wyif on RS		pattern repeat
V	sl 1 wyif on WS		

Center Back Panel

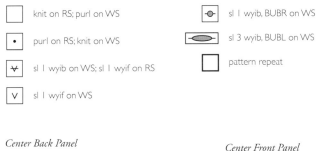

Center Front Panel

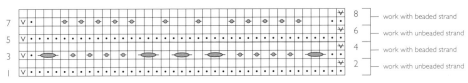

Row 2: (RS) Rep Row 1.

Row 3: (bead row, WS) With beaded strand, sl 1 st wyif, k1, sl 3 sts wyib, BUBL, [p1, sl 1 st wyib, BUBR] 4 times, p1, [sl 3 sts wyib, BUBL, p1] 3 times, [sl 1 st wyib, BUBR, p1] 4 times, sl 3 sts wyib, BUBL, k2.

Row 4: With beaded strand, sl 1 st wyif, knit to end, but do not bring up any beads.

Rows 5 and 6: With unbeaded strand, Rep Row 1.

Row 7: (bead row, WS) With beaded strand. Sl 1 st wyif, k1, p3, [sl 1 st wyib, BUBR, p1] 4 times, [sl 1 st wyib, BUBR, p3] 3 times, [sl 1 st wyib, BUBR, p1] 4 times, sl 1 st wyib, BUBR, p3, k2.

Row 8: With beaded strand, sl 1 st wyif, knit to end, but do not bring up any beads.

Repeat Rows 1–8 from chart or as above, 25 (25, 26, 27) more times, then work the first 0 (6, 4, 2) rows of the pattern once more—208 (214, 220, 226) pattern rows; 26 (27, 28, 28) long bead rows. Knit 4 rows, slipping the first st of each row wyif—piece measures about 17½ (18, 18½, 19)" (44.5 [45.5, 47, 48.5] cm) from beg. BO as if to knit on next WS row.

Left Side Panel

Prestring one strand with 101 (104, 107, 110) each round and long beads as follows: [1 round bead, 1 long bead] 101 (104, 107, 110) times. Use these beads before the armhole shaping.

Position both center back and front panels in front of you with RS facing, front panel on the right and back panel on the left. With unbeaded strand, pick up and knit 92 (95, 98, 101) sts evenly spaced along left edge of center front panel, beg at the CO edge, and ending at the BO edge; CO 15 (15, 15, 16) sts for neck opening; pick up and knit 98 (101, 104, 106) sts evenly spaced along left edge of center

back panel—205 (211, 217, 223) sts. Knit 2 rows, slipping the first st of each row with yarn in front (wyif). Work for 38 (40, 42, 46) rows in pattern from side panel chart, ending with Row 6 (8, 10, 12)—piece measures about 3¾ (4, 4¼, 4½)" (9.5 [10, 11, 11.5] cm) from pick up row. Rows 1–32 are written out in words as follows:

Row 1: (WS) With unbeaded strand, sl 1 st wyif, knit to end.

Row 2: (RS) Rep Row 1.

Row 3: (bead row, WS) With beaded strand, sl 1 st wyif, k1, *sl 3 sts wyib, BUBL, p1, sl 1 st wyib, BUBR, p1; rep from * to last 5 sts, sl 3 sts wyib, BUBL, k2.

Row 4: With beaded strand, sl 1 st wyif, knit to end, but do not bring up any beads.

Rows 5 and 6: With unbeaded strand, rep Row 1.

Row 7: With unbeaded strand, sl 1 st wyif, k1, purl to last 2 sts, k2.

Rows 8–10: With unbeaded strand, rep Row 1.

Row 11: With unbeaded strand, sl 1 st wyif, k1, *p1, sl 1 st wyib; rep from * to last 3 sts, p1, k2.

Rows 12–14: With unbeaded strand, rep Row 1.

Side Panel

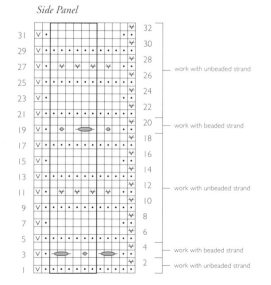

Row 15: With unbeaded strand, rep Row 7.

Rows 16–18: With unbeaded strand, rep Row 1.

Row 19: (bead row, WS) With beaded strand, sl 1 st wyif, k1, *p1, sl 1 st wyib, BUBR, p1, sl 3 sts wyib, BUBL; rep from * to last 5 sts, p1, sl 1 st wyib, BUBR, p1, k2.

Row 20: With beaded strand, sl 1 st wyif, knit to end, but do not bring up any beads.

Rows 21 and 22: With unbeaded strand, rep Row 1.

Row 23: With unbeaded strand, rep Row 7.

Rows 24–26: With unbeaded strand, rep Row 1.

Row 27: With unbeaded strand, sl 1 st wyif, k1, *p1, sl 1 st wyib; rep from * to last 3 sts, p1, k2.

Rows 28–30: With unbeaded strand, rep Row 1.

Row 31: With unbeaded strand, rep Row 7.

Row 32: With unbeaded strand, rep Row 1.

Repeat Rows 1–32 for pattern.

Shape armholes: On the next row (WS), keeping in pattern as established, work across first 65 (68, 72, 77) sts, BO the next 75 (75, 73, 69) sts for armhole, work in patt to end. Prestring 2 strands, one for each side section, with 11 (13, 25, 42) each round and long beads as follows: [1 long bead, 1 round bead] 11 (13, 25, 42) times. Use these beads during and after the armhole shaping. *Note:* This is probably more beads than you will need, but it is better to have too many prepared than too few. Take notice of how many beads you have left on the strand when you finish, and use that number to determine how many beads were actually used for the side panel; then you can top up the strand with the unused beads for the other side panel.

Working each side separately with its own beaded and unbeaded strands, and keeping 3 sts at each armhole edge in unbeaded St st for selvedges, work decs as follows: (RS) Work to last 3 sts of first section, k2tog, k1; at beg of second section k1, ssk, work to end—64 (67, 71, 76) sts in

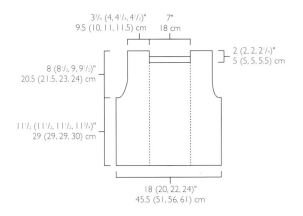

each section. Rep the dec row every RS row 4 (7, 10, 14) more times—60 (60, 61, 62) sts in each section. Keeping in patt, work even until piece measures 5½ (6½, 7½, 8½)" (14 [16.5, 19, 21.5] cm) from pickup row, and end having just completed a RS row. Transfer sts for each side to a separate spare needle. With WS facing and RS of pieces touching each other, use three-needle bind-off or Kitchener grafting to join live sts of sides tog.

Right Side Panel

Prestring one strand as for left-side panel. Position center back and front panels in front of you with RS facing, back panel on the right and front panel on the left. With unbeaded strand, pick up and knit 98 (101, 104, 106) sts evenly spaced along right edge of center back panel, CO 15 (15, 15, 16) sts for neck opening, pick up and knit 92 (95, 98, 101) sts evenly spaced along right edge of center front panel—205 (211, 217, 223) sts. Complete as for left side panel.

Finishing

Block pieces to measurements. Work 2 or 3 rows of single crochet evenly around neck opening, armholes, and along bottom edge. Weave in ends.

CHAPTER 4

Beaded Knitting:
Prestrung, Knitted through Stitches
Vargas Girl Pullover

One can actually knit a prestrung bead *through* the actual stitch. After inserting the needle into the stitch, as you wrap the yarn around the needle, snuggle the bead up to the junction between the two needles, then knit both the yarn and bead through the stitch. I have found that using the left index finger (knitting) or the left thumb (purling) helps to push the bead through when you're working the stitch.

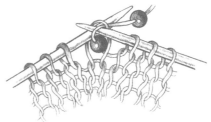

Bead knit through stitch

Notice how the bead can fall to either the right or wrong side of the fabric. This is because the bead may follow the path of the actual looped stitch itself. Thus it may sit on either "leg" of a stitch.

To make sure the bead does not jump around, and to cover up the stitch evenly, work the stitch that the bead is on through its *back loop* on the subsequent row.

To knit a bead, stitch through back loop; make sure the bead is to the right side (or in front of the needle). Insert the right needle tip in the back of the stitch and knit. To purl a bead, stitch through back loop; make sure the bead is to the right side (or in back of the needle). Insert the right needle tip in the back of the stitch, make sure the needle tip is above the bead, and purl.

Bead purl through stitch

The bead now lies on a diagonal like needlepoint stitches, or the earth on its axis. Repeat this beading process on each and every stitch and you have the basis of true Bead Knitting.

Knit bead stitch through back loop

Purl bead stitch through back loop

Bead position possibilities

Vargas Girl Pullover

Sometimes, a pattern that's too repetitious gets boring. In this pullover, notice how I avoid this by clustering the beads close together at the bottom, only to disperse them as they get to the top. Worked in a sinfully luxurious cashmere blend, the sweater has a feel that's too yummy to resist. To keep costs down, I've made this a short-sleeved top, but feel free to go all out and make longer sleeves (perhaps the fresh three-quarters length just past the elbow). If the cashmere cost is prohibitive, substitute Jaeger's Matchmaker Merino in the same weight.

Finished Size

34 (37, 40½, 44)" (86.5 [94, 103, 112] cm) bust/chest circumference. Top shown measures 37" (94 cm). This garment is intended to be standard-fitting.

Materials

- Yarn: Jaeger Cashmina (80% cashmere, 20% extra fine Merino wool; 135 yd [123 m]/25 g): #042 verdigris (pale green), 8 (9, 10, 11) skeins. Yarn distributed by Westminster Fibers.

- Beads: Size 6 or 10mm seed beads: about 2,850 (3,150, 3,350, 3,750). Shown in frosted grape, from Beads World.

- Needles: Size 3 (3.25 mm): straight or 24" (60-cm) circular (cir) and 16" (40-cm) circular (cir). Adjust needle size if necessary to obtain the correct gauge.

- Notions: Bead-stringing needle; stitch markers; tapestry needle.

Gauge

29 sts and 41 rows = 4" (10 cm) in St st.

Special Notes

Prestring beads on yarn before working.

Work from two separate balls of yarn, one with pre-strung beads and one without beads. When you are ready to work a WS beading row, change to the beaded strand. Work the following RS row from the beaded strand, but do not bring up any beads. Change back to the strand without beads and work the plain rows between the beaded rows as required.

When there is a long interval without beads, carry the beaded strand along the selvedge, catching the unused strand every few rows by twisting the two strands together to prevent a long float on the sides (see illustration at right).

Catching the yarn not in use at the edge

When you're working the neckband in the round, work beads into knit stitches on the RS of the neckband. On the foll round, work each beaded stitch through its back loop as usual.

Special Abbreviations

BP1: Bead Purl 1. On a WS row, purl the stitch to be beaded, making sure the bead gets pushed through the stitch along with the yarn. In this way, the bead is also purled through the stitch.

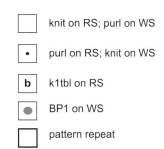

knit on RS; purl on WS

· purl on RS; knit on WS

b k1tbl on RS

● BP1 on WS

pattern repeat

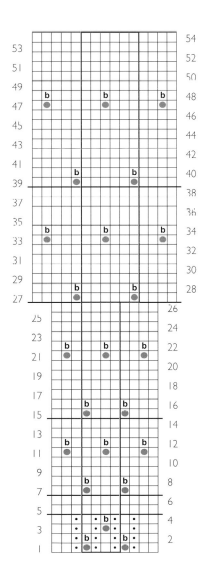

BK1: Bead Knit 1 (used for neckband). On a RS round, knit the st to be beaded, making sure the bead gets pushed through the stitch along with the yarn.

Back

Ribbing: Prestring about 413 (455, 497, 525) beads on one strand of yarn. CO 123 (135, 147, 155) sts, and work setup row without beads as follows: (RS) K2, *p1, k1; rep from * to last 3 sts, end p1, k2. Change to ribbing pattern from chart; Rows 1–4 are written out in words as follows:

Row 1: (WS) P2, k1, *BP1, k1, p1, k1; rep from * to last 4 sts, end BP1, k1, p2.

Row 2: (RS) K2, p1, k1tbl, *p1, k1, p1, k1tbl; rep from * to last 3 sts, end p1, k2.

Row 3: P2, k1, *p1, k1, BP1, k1; rep from * to last 4 sts, end p1, k1, p2.

Row 4: K2, p1, k1, *p1, k1tbl, p1, k1; rep from * to last 3 sts, end p1, k2.

Repeat Rows 1–4 six more times—29 rows total, including the setup row; piece measures about 2¾" (7 cm) from beg. Work 2 rows St st without beads (Rows 5 and 6 of chart).

Body: Prestring about 541 (612, 624, 749) beads on one strand of yarn. Using the beaded and unbeaded strands as given in Special Notes, cont in pattern from chart; Rows 7–14 are written out in words as follows:

Row 7: P3, *BP1, p3; rep from * to end.

Row 8: *K3, k1tbl; rep from * to last 3 sts, end k3.

Rows 9 and 10: Work in St st (knit on RS, purl on WS).

Row 11: P1, BP1, p1, *p2, BP1, p1; rep from * to last 4 sts, p2, BP1, p1.

Row 12: *K1, k1tbl, k2; rep from * to last 3 sts, end k1, k1tbl, k1.

Rows 13 and 14: Work in St st.

Repeat Rows 7–14 two more times—piece measures about 5¼" (13.5 cm) from beg.

Cont in pattern from chart; Rows 15–26 are written out in words as follows:

Row 15: P3 *BP1, p3; rep from * to end.

Row 16: *K3, k1tbl; rep from * to last 3 sts, end k3.

Rows 17–20: Work in St st.

Row 21: P1, BP1, p1, *p2, BP1, p1; rep from * to last 4 sts, p2, BP1, p1.

Row 22: *K1, k1tbl, k2; rep from * to last 3 sts, end k1, k1tbl, k1.

Rows 23–26: Work in St st.

Repeat Rows 15–26 two more times, increasing 0 (0, 0, 4) sts in last row—123 (135, 147, 159) sts; piece measures about 8¾" (22 cm) from beg.

Cont in pattern from chart; Rows 27–38 are written out in words as follows:

Row 27: P4, BP1, *p5, BP1; rep from * to last 4 sts, end p4.

Row 28: K4, *k1tbl, k5; rep from * to last 5 sts, end k1tbl, k4.

Rows 29–32: Work in St st.

Row 33: P1, BP1, p3, *p2, BP1, p3; rep from * to last 4 sts, end p2, BP1, p1.

Row 34: K1, k1tbl, k2, *k3, k1tbl, k2; rep from * to last 5 sts, end k3, k1tbl, k1.

Rows 35–38: Work in St st.

Repeat Rows 27–35 one more time—piece measures about 10¾" (27.5 cm) from beg.

Shape armholes: BO 6 (7, 7, 9) sts at the beg of the next 2 rows (Rows 36 and 37 of chart)—111 (121, 133, 141) sts. On the next row (Row 38 of chart), work fully fashioned decreases as follows: K2, k2tog, work to last 4 sts, ssk, k2—109 (119, 131, 139) sts.

Mark center 99 (111, 123, 135) sts for pattern placement and establish patt from Rows 39–54 of chart over the marked center sts (see rows in words below), and work sts at each side in St st. At the same time, cont armhole shaping by working fully fashioned decreases as above every RS row 3 (4, 7, 7) more times, then every fourth row twice—99 (107, 113, 121) sts rem when armhole shaping has been completed; remove markers when necessary. Rows 39–54 are written out in words as follows:

Row 39: P4, BP1, *p5, BP1; rep from * to last 4 sts, end p4.

Row 40: K4, *k1tbl, k5; rep from * to last 5 sts, end k1tbl, k4.

Rows 41–46: Work in St st.

Row 47: P1, BP1, p3, *p2, BP1, p3; rep from * to last 4 sts, end p2, BP1, p1.

Row 48: K1, k1tbl, k2, *k3, k1tbl, k2; rep from * to last 5 sts, end k3, k1tbl, k1.

Rows 49–54: Work in St st.

Note: The patt from Rows 39–54 will be worked as established to the end of the piece.

Rep Rows 39–54 until armholes measure 5¾ (6¼, 6¾, 7¼)" (14.5 [16, 17, 18.5] cm), and end having just completed a RS row.

Shape back neck and shoulders: Cont in patt, work 34 (38, 40, 44) sts, BO center 31 (31, 33, 33) sts, join a separate ball of yarn, work in patt to end—34 (38, 40, 44) sts at each side. Working each side separately in patt, BO at each neck edge 6 sts once, 4 sts once, then 2 sts once—22 (26, 28, 32) sts at each side. *Note:* The rest of the neck shaping and shoulder shaping are worked at the same time; read the next section through to the end before proceeding. Dec 1 st fully fashioned at each side of neck opening on the next 3 RS rows as follows: On first shoulder work to last 4 sts, ssk, k2; on second shoulder k2, k2tog, work to end—3 sts decreased from each side of neck when all neck decreases have been completed. At the same time, when armholes measure 6½ (7, 7½, 8)" (16.5 [18, 19, 20.5] cm), work shoulder shaping by BO at each armhole edge 4 (5, 5, 6) sts 4 (3, 3, 4) times, then BO at each armhole edge 0 (4, 5, 0) sts once—3 (4, 5, 5) sts rem at each side. BO rem sts at beg of next RS row for first shoulder, or at beg of next WS row for second shoulder.

Front

Work same as back until armholes measure 4¼ (4¾, 5¼, 5¾)" (11 [12, 13.5, 14.5] cm); end having just completed a RS row—99 (107, 113, 121) sts.

Shape front neck and shoulders: Cont in patt as established, work 35 (39, 41, 45) sts, BO center 29 (29, 31, 31) sts, join a separate ball of yarn with beads on it (with about the same number of beads as on other side), work in patt to end—35 (39, 41, 45) sts at each side. Working each side separately in patt, BO at each neck edge 4 sts once, 3 sts once, then 2 sts once—26 (30, 32, 36) sts at each side. *Note:* The rest of the neck shaping and shoulder shaping are worked at the same time; read the next section through to the end before proceeding. Working fully fashioned decreases as for back neck, dec 1 st at each side of neck opening on the next 5 RS rows, then every other RS row (every 4 rows) twice. At the same time, when armholes measure 6½ (7, 7½, 8)" (16.5 [18, 19, 20.5] cm), work shoulder shaping as for back.

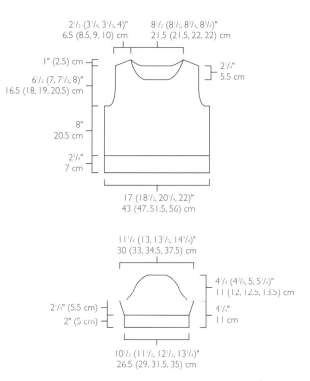

Sleeves

Ribbing: Prestring about 296 (336, 370, 408) beads on one strand of yarn for each sleeve. CO 75 (83, 91, 99) sts, and work setup row without beads as follows: (RS) K2, *p1, k1; rep from * to last 3 sts, end p1, k2. Repeat Rows 1–4 of chart as for back a total of five times—21 rows total, including the setup row; piece measures about 2" (5 cm) from beg. Purl 1 row on WS (Row 5 of chart). *Note:* The sleeve shaping and pattern changes are worked at the same time; read the next section through to the end before proceeding. Beg with the next RS row (Row 6 of chart), work fully fashioned increases as follows every 4 rows 5 (5, 2, 2) times, then every 6 rows 0 (0, 2, 2) times: K2, M1 (see Abbreviations), work in patt to last 2 sts, M1, k2—85 (93, 99, 107) sts when all increases have been completed. At the same time, work beaded patt as follows until piece measures 4¼" (11 cm) from beg, and end having just completed a WS row: Work Rows 7–38 straight through one time (without repeating any sections), then repeat Rows 39–54 as required to end.

Shape sleeve cap: Cont in patt, BO 6 (7, 7, 7) sts at the beg of the next 2 rows—73 (79, 85, 93) sts. Dec 1 st fully fashioned at each side of the next 17 (19, 21, 22) RS rows as follows: K2, k2tog, work in patt to last 4 sts, ssk, k2—39 (41, 43, 49) sts. Work 1 row on WS. BO 2 sts at the beg of the next 2 rows, then BO 3 sts at the beg of the next 2 rows, then BO 4 sts at the beg of the next 2 rows—21 (23, 25, 31) sts. BO rem sts on next RS row.

Finishing

Weave in ends. Block pieces to measurements. Sew shoulder seams. Set sleeves in armholes. Sew sleeve and side seams.

Neckband

Prestring about 234 (234, 240, 240) beads. Using cir needle and RS facing, and beg at right shoulder seam, pick up and knit 71 (71, 73, 73) sts across back neck, then pick up and knit 85 (85, 87, 87) sts evenly across front neck—156 (156, 160, 160) sts. Place marker to indicate beg of round (rnd). Working in the rnd with the RS of piece facing you at all times, work setup rnd of neckband ribbing as follows: *K1, p1; rep from * around. Work beaded ribbing in the rnd as follows:
Rnd 1: *BK1, p1, k1, p1; rep from * around.
Rnd 2: *K1tbl, p1, k1, p1; rep from * around.
Rnd 3: *K1, p1, BK1, p1; rep from * around.
Rnd 4: *K1, p1, k1tbl, p1; rep from * around.

Repeat Rnds 1–4 twice more—13 rnds total, including the setup rnd; neckband measures about 1¼" (3.2 cm). On the next rnd, BO all sts loosely in ribbing. Weave in ends.

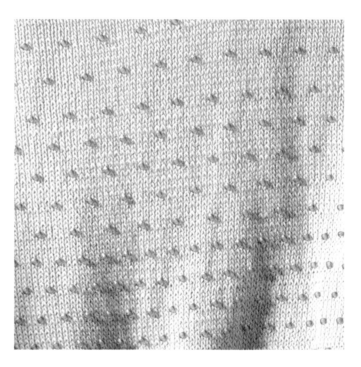

CHAPTER 5

Bead Knitting: Prestrung,
Knitted through Stitches
Floral Beaded Pockets

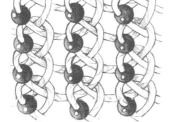

Throwing the yarn opposite direction in knit

Throwing the yarn opposite direction in purl

As described in Chapters 1 and 4, true Bead Knitting, with stockinette stitch as its base, entails two premises: that a bead is actually worked through all stitches, and that every stitch is subsequently secured on the following row by working through its back loop.

There is an inherent problem with this allover bead fabric. As in the needlepoint that it emulates, the fabric's nature is to bias or torque.

To alleviate this tendency, you can alternate the twist of the stitch with each row. Typically, working a stitch through its back loop twists the stitch below it to the left (see illustration at top left). To create a stitch that is twisted in the opposite direction (or to the right), throw the yarn in the opposite direction on the previous row.

This is known as the Eastern or Oriental method. On the subsequent row, working normally into the stitch with the twist opposite from normal creates the right slant. Working into the back loop of this stitch with the twist opposite from normal creates a regular fabric with no twist (often referred to as Eastern Uncrossed Knitting). A fabric of only these right-twisted stitches (pictured at the top of page 40) is the exact mirror image of the left-twisted stitches with beads pictured at top left on this page.

In what is sometimes referred to as Plaited Knitting, a row of left-twisted stitches alternates with a row of right-twisted stitches. This alternation almost creates a herringbone effect. See example on page 40.

Do not forget, however, that this maneuvering occurs while beads are worked through the stitches at the same time! Thus, here is a summary for knitting circularly in the round as well as back and forth, and for a fabric that twists left only as well as for plaited fabric.

Working back and forth, with left twists only:

Row 1: (RS) Knit normally, pushing a bead through each and every stitch.

A fabric of bead knitting with all stitches worked through back loops

Row 2: (WS) Purl through back loop, pushing a bead through every stitch, making sure beads of previous row fall to the back of the work, which is the right side.

Row 3: Knit through back loop, pushing a bead through every stitch, making sure beads of previous row fall to the front of the work.

Repeat Rows 2 and 3.

Right-twisted fabric

Working circularly with left twists only:

Round 1: Same as Row 1 above.

Round 2: Same as Row 3 above.

Repeat Round 2.

Plaited fabric

Working back and forth with alternating twists:

Row 1: (RS) Same as Row 1 above but knit throwing yarn in opposite direction.

Row 2: (WS) Purl throwing yarn in the normal way (the way the yarn was thrown in the previous row ensures that the twist will be the opposite from the method through the back loop), pushing a bead through every stitch. Make sure that the beads of previous row fall to the back (or right side) of work.

Row 3: Knit through back loop, pushing a bead through every stitch, making sure beads of the previous row fall to the front of the work while you throw the yarn in the opposite direction.

Repeat Rows 2 and 3.

Working circularly with alternating twists:

Round 1: Same as Row 1 above, but knit throwing yarn in opposite direction.

Round 2: Knit throwing yarn in the normal way (the way the yarn was thrown in the previous row ensures that the twist will be the opposite from the method through the back loop), pushing a bead through every stitch. Make sure that the beads of the previous row fall to the front (or right side) of work.

Round 3: Knit through back loop, pushing a bead through every stitch. Make sure that the beads of the previous row fall to the front of the work; throw yarn in opposite direction.

Repeat Rounds 2 and 3.

True Bead Knitting is most often used in purses and is typically worked in the round or circularly. You follow a chart, not unlike that for Fair Isle knitting or stranded

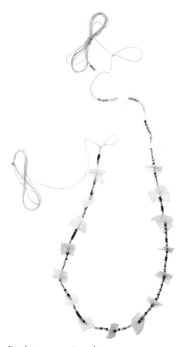

Beads strung up in order

color work patterns. The difference, however, is that the beads must be strung up in exact reverse order! The beads create the patterning.

Since there is a bead on each stitch, great care must be given to the precision of the beading sequence. The last bead strung on the yarn is the first to appear in the process of knitting the yarn. If there is a mistake in the beading sequence, the yarn must be cut and the beads restrung. I have had luck breaking off an offending bead (if it is an extra one) carefully with pliers. I also string on a small piece of paper between rows to keep me on track. My good friend Barbara Hillery suggests that if you're missing beads, just work the stitches without beads, then go back and sew beads with a needle and thread over the bare areas.

She also suggests that if a bead is the wrong color (that is, you made a mistake in the beading sequence), a little dab of the correct color nail polish can save you from having to cut the yarn and restring! Barbara is soooo smart.

When you're following the chart, place arrows on each row in the direction of the knitting. Begin at the bottom. If you're working back and forth flat, the arrows will reverse direction with each row.

Circular knitting in the round means that you work all rows from right to left. Thus, string the beads from the top of the chart down, and always read from left to right down.

Thread is typically used, as are fine needles (size 0 and smaller). As seen in Chapter 1, the thread is not seen from the right side. True Bead Knitting is not for the faint-hearted, but its luxurious fabric is like no other. Certainly, it should be tried once, if just in small ways. For this reason, I offer a pattern for a floral pocket. Attach it to an existing sweater or use the chart to create a matching sweater with the intarsia method and many different colors of yarn.

To compare and contrast methods, one pocket, worked back and forth flat, is done in left-twist stitches. The second pocket is worked in alternating plaits. The third pocket employs the first "between-the-stitches" method.

Notice how the gauge of the latter is radically altered. The stitch gauge widens and the row gauge condenses. Thus, use of the same chart can produce a short wide picture. Notice how the bead pattern reads better in the version that twists left only. The plaited version lacks bias, but does not have the same pictorial definition.

In stringing the beads, you may find it easier to determine the color of the beads from the knitting chart or from the colors written out in words.

Floral Beaded Pockets

When a true, allover Bead Knitting project seems too daunting, think small. After all, good things come in small packages. A floral pattern is interpreted in three ways here. The plaited version is probably the most desirable, but choose a version that jibes with your own visual and knitting preferences. Or try two of the methods on separate pieces, then seam them together along three sides. Add a strap, maybe a zipper across the top, and create a change purse!

Finished Size
About 5" (12.5 cm) wide and 3¼" (8.5 cm) high.

Materials
- Yarn: Skacel Manuela Size 10 (100% cotton; 308 yd [282 m]/50 g): #M061 creme, 1 skein for all three projects.

- Beads: Size 11 silver-lined glass seed beads, in the colors and amounts shown below. Beads shown from Sandaga, style number not available.

- About 1,150 white (W); 100 light green (LG); 125 each medium green (MG) and dark green (DG); 125 light red (LR); 75 each medium red (MR) and dark red (DR); 60 light blue (LB); 40 each medium blue (MB) and dark blue (DB); 50 each light yellow (LY), medium yellow (MY), and dark yellow (DY).

- Needles: Size 0000 (1.25 mm): straight or double-pointed. Adjust needle size if necessary to obtain the correct gauge.

- Notions: Bead-stringing needle; small tapestry needle.

Gauge
30 sts and 60 rows = 4" (10 cm) in Bead Knitting. Exact gauge is not critical for this project.

Special Notes
Beads are strung in the reverse order that they will be knitted. In other words, the first bead strung will be the last bead used for knitting, and the last bead strung will be the first bead used for knitting. Compare the illustrations on pages 46 and 47.

You may find it helpful to place a small piece of scrap paper or other marker on the beaded strand to indicate the beginning and end of each row.

Special Abbreviations
BUB: Bring Up Bead, snuggle the bead up close to the needle. Each bead will lie on the yarn strand between two stitches.

Bead Stringing Order for All Pockets
Prestring beads for each pocket in the following order, or according to the diagram on page 47:

Stringing Row 1: 38 W.

Row 2: 5 W, 2 DG, 4 W, 2 MG, 17 W, 3 DG, 5 W.

Row 3: 4 W, 1 MG, 1 W, 1 MG, 2 LG, 15 W, 4 MG, 2 W, 1 DG, 2 W, 1 MG, 2 W, 1 MG, 1 W.

Row 4: 1 W, 4 MG, 3 W, 1 DG, 1 W, 1 MG, 3 W, 1 MG, 3 W, 3 MR, 3 DR, 4 W, 1 LG, 2 MG, 7 W.

Row 5: 2 W, 1 MG, 5 W, 2 LG, 2 W, 1 MR, 1 DR, 2 MR,

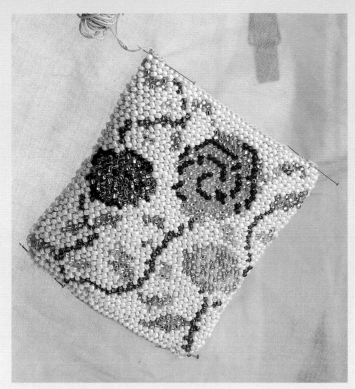

Alternating Twist Pocket

Left Twist Pocket

Between the Stitches Pocket

3 LR, 3 MR, 6 W, 1 DG, 5 W, 2 MG, 2 W.

Row 6: 6 W, 1 LG, 3 W, 1 DG, 5 W, 3 MR, 3 LR, 2 MR,
1 DR, 1 MR, 2 W, 1 LG, 5 W, 2 MG, 2 W.

Row 7: 2 W, 3 MG, 4 W, 2 LG, 1 MR, 1 DR, 1 MR,
2 LR, 6 DR, 5 W, 1 DG, 2 W, 2 LG, 6 W.

Row 8: 7 W, 1 LG, 1 W, 2 DG, 4 W, 1 DR, 6 LR, 1 DR,
2 LR, 1 DR, 1 MR, 1 LG, 4 W, 1 MG, 1 LG, 2 MG,
2 W.

Row 9: 3 W, 2 MG, 1 LG, 1 MG, 4 W, 1 MR, 1 DR,
2 LR, 1 DR, 6 LR, 1 DR, 5 W, 3 DG, 7 W.

Row 10: 6 W, 2 DG, 2 W, 1 MG, 3 W, 1 DR, 2 LR, 4 DR,
2 LR, 1 DR, 2 LR, 1 DR, 1 LR, 3 W, 1 MG, 1 LG,
1 MG, 4W.

Row 11: 5 W, 2 MG, 3 W, 1 DR, 2 LR, 1 DR, 2 LR,
1 DR, 4 LR, 1 DR, 2 LR, 1 DR, 1 W, 2 MG, 3 W,
2 DG, 5 W.

Row 12: 4 W, 2 DG, 4 W, 2 MG, 1 W, 1 DR, 2 LR, 1 DR,
4 LR, 1 DR, 2 LR, 1 DR, 2 LR, 1 DR, 3 W, 1 DG,
6 W.

Row 13: 6 W, 1 DG, 3 W, 1 DR, 2 LR, 1 DR, 1 LR,
1 MR, 2 LR, 1 DR, 3 LR, 1 DR, 1 LR, 1 DR, 1 W,
1 MG, 4 W, 1 LG, 2 W, 1 DG, 3 W.

Row 14: 3 W, 1 DG, 2 W, 2 LG, 5 W, 1 MR, 1 DR, 3 LR,
1 DR, 2 LR, 1 MR, 2 LR, 1 DR, 1 LR, 1 MR, 1 DR,
2 W, 1 DG, 7 W.

Row 15: 3 W, 1 LG, 3 W, 1 DG, 2 W, 1 LR, 1 DR, 2 LR,
2 DR, 3 LR, 1 DR, 1 LR, 1 MR, 1 LR, 1 DR, 1 MR,
5 W, 1 LG, 3 W, 1 DG, 3 W.

Row 16: 3 W, 1 DG, 9 W, 1 MR, 1 DR, 1 LR, 1 MR,
1 LR, 1 DR, 3 LR, 2 DR, 2 LR, 1 DR, 1 LR, 2 W,
1 DG, 3 W, 2 LG, 2 W.

Row 17: 2 W, 3 LG, 2 W, 1 DG, 3 W, 2 MR, 3 LR, 3 DR,
2 LR, 1 MR, 1 LR, 10 W, 1 DG, 4 W.

Row 18: 5 W, 1 DG, 4 DB, 5 W, 1 DR, 1 LR, 1 MR,

6 LR, 2 MR, 4 W, 1 DG, 1 W, 3 LG, 3 W.

Row 19: 6 W, 1 DG, 5 W, 2 MR, 6 LR, 1 MR, 1 LR,
1 DR, 4 W, 2 DB, 3 LB, 1 MB, 5 W.

Row 20: 3 W, 2 DB, 2 LB, 2 MB, 2 LB, 1 MB, 4 W, 2 DR,
2 MR, 1 LR, 4 MR, 1 W, 2 LG, 3 W, 1 DG, 6 W.

Row 21: 5 W, 1 DG, 3 W, 3 LG, 3 W, 5 MR, 5 W, 1 MB,
2 LB, 1 MB, 2 LB, 2 MB, 1 LB, 2 DB, 2 W.

Row 22: 2 W, 1 DB, 1 LB, 1 MB, 2 LB, 2 DB, 1 LB, 1 DB,
1 LB, 1 MB, 5 W, 5 MR, 4 W, 3 LG, 3 W, 1 DG, 4 W.

Row 23: 3 W, 1 DG, 12 W, 1 DG, 8 W, 1 MB, 1 LB,
1 DB, 3 LB, 1 DB, 1 LB, 1 MB, 1 LB, 1 DB, 2 W.

Row 24: 2 W, 1 DB, 1 LB, 1 MB, 2 LB, 2 MB, 3 LB,
1 DB, 8 W, 1 DG, 5 W, 1 LY, 1 MY, 3 LY, 3 W, 1 DG,
2 W.

Row 25: 2 W, 1 DG, 2 W, 4 DY, 3 MY, 5 W, 1 DG, 8 W,
1 MB, 2 LB, 1 MB, 2 LB, 1 MB, 2 LB, 3 W.

Row 26: 3 W, 1 DB, 1 LB, 1 MB, 1 LB, 1 MB, 2 LB,
2 MB, 3 W, 2 MG, 3 W, 1 DG, 4 W, 1 MY, 2 LY, 2
DY, 2 LY, 2 MY, 1 W, 1 DG, 2 W.

Row 27: 3 W, 2 MY, 1 LY, 3 DY, 3 LY, 2 MY, 3 W, 2 DG,
1 W, 4 MG, 3 W, 1 MB, 2 LB, 2 MB, 2 LB, 1 DB,
3 W.

Row 28: 4 W, 2 DB, 2 LB, 2 DB, 4 W, 1 MG, 3 W, 1 MG,
1 DG, 4 W, 1 MY, 1 LY, 1 DY, 1 LY, 1 DY, 1 LY,
2 MY, 1 DY, 1 LY, 2 MY, 2 W.

Row 29: 2 W, 1 MY, 2 LY, 1 DY, 1 MY, 1 LY, 1 DY, 1 MY,
2 LY, 1 DY, 1 MY, 1 DY, 3 W, 1 DG, 10 W, 4 DB,
5 W.

Row 30: 5 W, 1 DG, 4 W, 1 MG, 8 W, 1 DG, 3 W, 2 DY,
1 MY, 1 LY, 1 DY, 3 LY, 1 MY, 1 DY, 2 LY, 1 DY, 2 W.

Row 31: 2 W, 2 MY, 2 LY, 1 DY, 2 MY, 1 DY, 1 LY, 2 MY,
1 DY, 4 W, 1 DG, 1 W, 1 MG, 6 W, 2 MG, 4 W,
1 DG, 4 W.

Row 32: 4 W, 1 DG, 3 W, 3 MG, 5 W, 1 MG, 1 W,

1 MG, 1 DG, 4 W, 2 DY, 2 MY, 5 LY, 2 MY, 3 W.

Row 33: 5 W, 4 MY, 1 LY, 3 DY, 5 W, 1 DG, 9 W, 2 MG, 2 W, 1 DG, 5 W.

Row 34: 6 W, 1 DG, 1 W, 1 MG, 10 W, 1 DG, 1 W, 2 LG, 4 W, 5 DY, 6 W.

Row 35: 3 W, 1 DG, 3 W, 1 DG, 6 W, 2 LG, 1 W, 2 DG, 4 W, 2 LG, 4 W, 2 DG, 7 W.

Row 36: 6 W, 1 MG, 2 W, 1 DG, 3 W, 1 LG, 1 MG, 2 LG, 3 W, 1 DG, 1 W, 2 LG, 7 W, 1 DG, 1 W, 1 DG, 4 W.

Row 37: 5 W, 1 DG, 9 W, 1 LG, 1 W, 1 DG, 3 W, 1 LG, 1 MG, 2 LG, 3 W, 1 DG, 2 W, 2 MG, 5 W.

Row 38: 5 W, 2 MG, 2 W, 1 DG, 4 W, 2 LG, 1 MG, 1 LG, 2 W, 1 DG, 11 W, 1 DG, 5 W.

Row 39: 5 W, 1 DG, 5 W, 1 LG, 5 W, 1 DG, 1 W, 2 LG, 1 MG, 2 LG, 4 W, 2 DG, 2 W, 1 MG, 5 W.

Row 40: 8 W, 1 DG, 6 W, 2 LG, 1 MG, 1 LG, 1 W, 1 DG, 4 W, 2 LG, 5 W, 1 DG, 5 W.

Row 41: 5 W, 1 DG, 5 W, 1 LG, 2 MG, 3 W, 2 DG, 2 LG, 8 W, 1 DG, 8 W.

Row 42: 7 W, 1 DG, 2 W, 2 LG, 7 W, 1 DG, 1 W, 1 MG 1 W, 1 MG, 2 LG, 3 W, 3 MG, 2 DG, 4 W.

Row 43: 4 W, 1 DG, 1 W, 1 MG, 2 LG, 1 MG, 3 W, 3 MG, 2 W, 2 DG, 6 W, 4 LG, 1 DG, 7 W.

Row 44: 3 W, 3 MG, 1 W, 1 DG, 1 W, 2 LG, 6 W, 2 DG, 8 W, 1 MG, 2 LG, 1 MG, 2 W, 1 DG, 4 W.

Row 45: 3 W, 2 DG, 2 W, 2 MG, 1 LG, 1 MG, 9 W, 5 DG, 5 W, 1 DG, 1 MG, 1 W, 1 MG, 2 LG, 2 W.

Row 46: 1 W, 1 LG, 2 MG, 4 W, 1 DG, 3 W, 1 DG, 13 W, 1 MG, 1 LG, 2 MG, 4 W, 1 DG, 3 W.

Row 47: 2 W, 2 DG, 6 W, 3 MG, 13 W, 1 DG, 1 W, 1 DG, 6 W, 2 LG, 1 W.

Row 48: 10 W, 1 DG, 25 W, 1 DG, 1 W.

Row 49: 38 W.

Left Twist Pocket

CO 40 sts. Knit the first and last st of every row without beads, keeping these edge sts loose so they will have the same tension as the rest of the work. Knitting begins on a WS or purl row (Row 1 of knitting chart).

Row 1: K1 (edge st), purl the next 38 sts normally without twisting, pushing a bead through each st, k1 (edge st).

Row 2: K1, knit the next 38 sts through the back loop (tbl), pushing a bead through each st, k1.

Row 3: K1, purl the next 38 sts tbl, pushing a bead through each st, making sure the beads of the previous row fall to the front (RS) of the work, k1.

Repeat Rows 2 and 3, alternating a RS row of working the beaded sts tbl with a WS row of purling the beaded sts tbl, until Row 49 has been completed. BO as if to knit tbl on the next row (RS).

Alternating Twist or Plaited Pocket

CO 40 sts. Knit the first and last st of every row without beads, keeping these edge sts loose so they will have the same tension as the rest of the work. Knitting begins on a WS or purl row (Row 1 of knitting chart).

Row 1: K1 (edge st), purl the next 38 sts normally without twisting, pushing a bead through each st, k1 (edge st).

Row 2: K1, knit the next 38 sts through the back loop (tbl) wrapping the yarn around the needle opposite the usual way and pushing a bead through each st, k1. Make sure the beads of the previous row fall to the front of the work (RS).

Row 3: K1, purl the next 38 sts normally, pushing bead through each st, making sure the beads of the previous row fall to the front (RS) of the work, k1.

Repeat Rows 2 and 3 until Row 49 has been completed. BO as if to knit tbl on the next row (RS).

Between the Stitches Pocket

CO 41 sts. Knitting begins on a WS or purl row (Row 1 of knitting chart).

Row 1: K2, *BUB, k1; rep from * to last st, end k1.

Row 2: K1, *p1, BUB; rep from * to last 2 sts, end p1, k1.

Repeat Rows 2 and 3 until Row 49 has been completed. BO as if to purl on the next row (RS).

Finishing

Weave in ends. Block piece if desired.

Beaded Pocket Knitting Chart

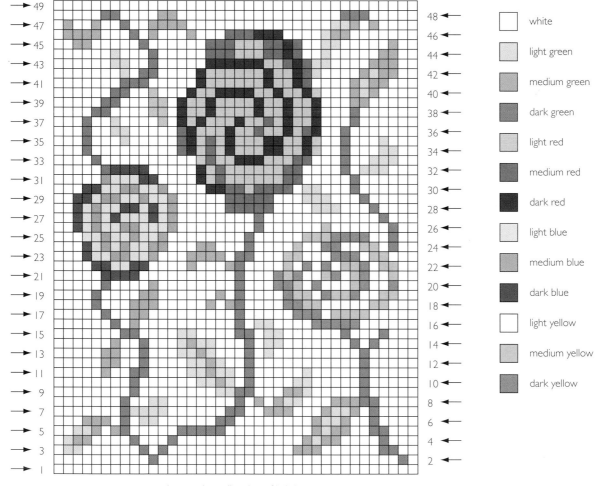

	white
	light green
	medium green
	dark green
	light red
	medium red
	dark red
	light blue
	medium blue
	dark blue
	light yellow
	medium yellow
	dark yellow

Arrows show direction of knitting

First bead strung,
last bead knit

Beaded Pocket Strung Beads

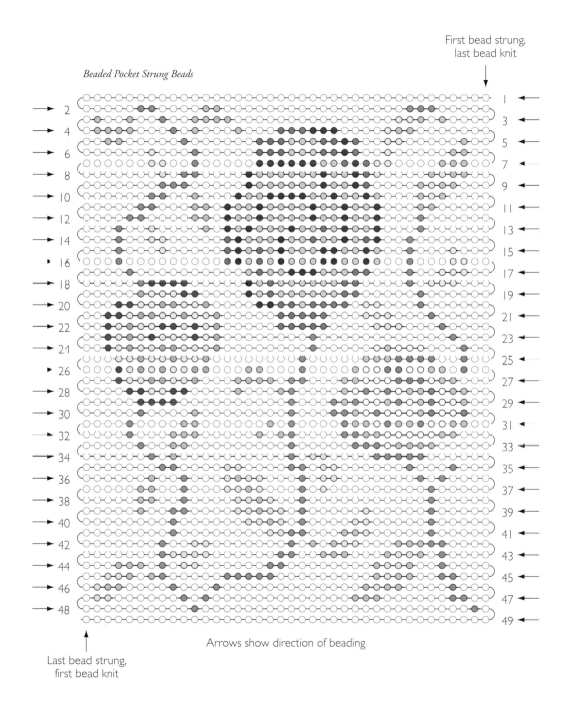

Arrows show direction of beading

Last bead strung,
first bead knit

CHAPTER 6

Beaded Knitting: Hoisted atop Stitches

Ethereal Lace Tunic, Bogus Bohus Cardigan

Hoisting beads atop stitches is one of my favorite methods of getting beads on knitting. I adapted the technique from machine knitting. It requires no pre-stringing, yet it is an integral part of the fabric. An unstrung bead is hoisted *atop* a whole stitch.

I use a special little latch hook called the American Beadle, which is actually a needle with a wooden handle used on a hosiery machine. You can also use any small, steel crochet hook meant for fine doilies.

Work up to the actual stitch that will hold the bead. Place the bead on the American Beadle or crochet hook. Take the stitch off the knitting needle and transfer it to the small hook.

Push the bead down onto the stitch until the whole stitch is pulled through the hole of the bead.

Place the stitch back on the knitting needle. It is now ready to be knitted or slipped as if to purl (not worked).

My preference is to slip the stitch because it forms a small float or strand behind the beaded stitch. Not only does this method make the bead stand out from the stitch, it protects the bead from skin oils and vice versa. There is nothing like the feel of cold beads against the body on a frigid, winter morning! Working the stitch does mean that the bead is positioned fully away from the needles, and eases the knitting process somewhat. It drops the bead down to a lower position and the bead is out of the way, so the stitch does not feel overly tight.

Whether you knitted or slipped the beaded stitch, note how it is now perfectly vertical. This means that beads with a clear direction will finally sit upright!

Bead on hook, stitch taken off

Stitch pulled through bead

Stitch ready to be either knitted or slipped

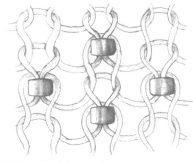

Fabric of hooked-on beads

Heart-shaped bead hoisted atop a stitch sits upright

The advantages of this method are many. It works in any stitch pattern. There is no abrasion on the yarn since there's no prestringing. The bead is very secure since both legs of a stitch—the two strands—hold it. Less-than-smooth yarn may be used. If you desire varying colors or types of beads, they do not have to be strung in exact order beforehand. Thus, one may add beads spontaneously—even whimsically—during the process. When you're working with more than one strand of yarn, each of the different yarns need not be prestrung. Furthermore, it is easy to add another color to a colorwork pattern without having to deal with more strands of yarn—just change the bead color! I use this method to attach shank buttons on buttonbands and to avoid sewing buttons on! (Can you tell I *really* like this method?)

Note: As a bonus, one of my favorite beaded cast-ons is included with the Ethereal Lace Tunic.

Ethereal Lace Tunic

To use the hooked-on-stitch method, you do interrupt the rhythm of knitting in order to get the hook out and place the bead on the stitch. This can be slightly more time consuming, so I've made the trims fancier with more beads, but used beads sparingly in the main body by continuing the beading in vertical lines here and there. This design results in a long, slimming visual effect. I see this tunic working beautifully as a bridal top for a casual wedding! In another color, it could work as a part of a bridesmaid's ensemble or as a lovely top for the mother of the bride or groom. For a less formal top, try substituting fun and funky beads in varied colors.

Finished Size
36 (40, 44, 48)" (91.5 [101.5, 112, 122] cm) bust/chest circumference. Top shown measures 40" (101.5 cm). This garment is intended to be loose fitting.

Materials
- Yarn: Crystal Palace Baby Georgia (100% cotton; 140 yd [128 m]/40 g): #0027 natural, 7 (8, 9, 10) skeins.

- Beads: Size 6 seed beads: about 1,800 (2,000, 2,200, 2,400). Shown in #0171 matte gold, from Beads World.

- Needles: Size 5 (3.75 mm): straight and 16" (40-cm) circular (cir). Adjust needle size if necessary to obtain the correct gauge.

- Notions: Bead-stringing needle; small steel crochet hook size 10 (1.25 mm) or smaller, or small bead hook; stitch markers; tapestry needle.

Gauge
24 sts and 34 rows = 4" (10 cm) in St st or beaded patt for body; 24 sts and 40 rows = 4" (10 cm) in lace trim patt.

Special Notes
In working the neckband in the round, work the trim beginning with Row 2, and work all WS rows as RS rounds by knitting all sts around.

Special Abbreviations
B1: Bead 1, worked on a RS row. Place bead on hook. Work to the stitch that will hold the bead, hook the top of the stitch, transfer the bead to the stitch by pushing it off the hook with your finger, and pull the top of the stitch up through the bead hole. Return the stitch to the left needle and slip it as if to purl with yarn in back.

Sk2p: Slip 1, k2tog, pass slipped st over. Slip the first st as if to knit, work the next 2 sts as k2tog, pass the slipped st over—2 sts decreased.

Yo: Yarnover. Wrap yarn over the needle as if to knit.

BUB: Bring Up Bead, snuggle the bead up close to the needle. Each bead will lie on the yarn strand between two stitches.

Back

Lace trim: CO 109 (121, 133, 145) sts using long-tailed cast-on with beads (see illustrations at right):

Reel off about 3 yd (3 m) of yarn, make a slipknot and place the yarn on the ndl. Prestring about 36 (40, 44, 48) beads on the short-tail strand, not the working strand coming from the ball of yarn. With tail yarn on thumb and working yarn on index finger, CO 1 st (2 sts on ndl). *BUB, CO3; rep from * until there are 107 (119, 131, 143) sts on ndl. BUB, CO 2 more sts—109 (121, 133, 145) sts total.

Work setup row without beads as follows: (WS) P2, knit to last 2 sts, end p2. Change to lace trim patt (Rows 1–8) from chart; Rows 1–8 are written out in words as follows:

Row 1: (RS) K2, *yo, sk2p, yo, sk2p; rep from * to last 5 sts, end yo, sk2p, yo, k2—75 (83, 91, 99) sts.

Row 2 and All WS Rows: Purl across.

Row 3: K2, *k1, place bead on next st and slip (sl) it as if to purl (purlwise) with yarn in back (wyib), k1, yo, k1, yo; rep from * to last 5 sts, end k1, place bead on next st and sl it purlwise wyib, k3—109 (121, 133, 145) sts.

Row 5: K2, *sk2p, yo, sk2p, yo; rep from * to last 5 sts, end sk2p, k2—73 (81, 89, 97) sts.

Row 7: K2, *yo, k1, yo, k1, place bead on next st and sl it purlwise wyib, k1; rep from * to last 3 sts, end yo, k1, yo, k2—109 (121, 133, 145) sts.

Row 8: Purl across.

Repeat Rows 1–8 five more times, then work Rows 1–4 once more—53 rows total, including the setup row; piece measures about 5¼" (13.5 cm) from beg; 109 (121, 133, 145) sts.

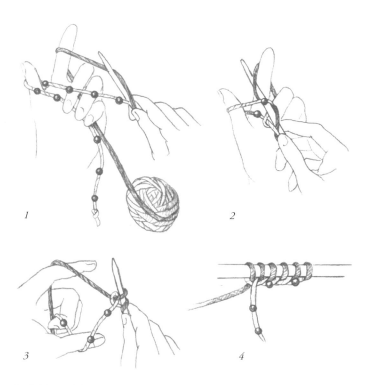

1 *2*

3 *4*

Beaded long-tailed cast-on

Body: Work body patt (Rows 9–12) from chart. Rows 9–12 are written out in words as follows:

Row 9: (RS) K5, *yo, sk2p, yo, k9; rep from * to last 8 sts, end yo, sk2p, yo, k5.

Rows 10 and 12: Purl across.

Row 11: K5, *k1, place bead on next st and sl it purlwise wyib, k10; rep from * to last 8 sts, end k1, place bead on next st and sl it purlwise wyib, k6.

Repeat Rows 9–12 until piece measures 14" (35.5 cm) from beg; end having just completed a WS row.

Shape armholes: Cont in patt, BO 4 (4, 5, 6) sts at the beg of the next 2 rows—101 (113, 123, 133) sts. *Note:* For all future shaping, if there are not at least 2 St sts on the outside of a yo/sk2p combination or a beaded st at the selvedge, omit the yo/sk2p or bead placement, and work those sts as St st instead. On the next RS row, work fully fashioned decreases as follows: K2, k2tog, work in patt to last 4 sts, ssk, k2—99 (111, 121, 131) sts. Work 1 WS row. Repeat the last 2 rows 4 (7, 9, 11) more times—91 (97, 103, 109) sts. Work even in patt until armholes measure 7½ (8, 8½, 9)" (19 [20.5, 21.5, 23] cm); end having just completed a RS row.

Shape back neck and shoulders: Neck and shoulder shaping are worked at the same time; read the next section through to the end before proceeding. Cont in patt, work 36 (39, 40, 42) sts, BO center 19 (19, 23, 25) sts, join a separate ball of yarn, work in patt to end—36 (39, 40, 42) sts at each side. Working each side separately in patt, BO at each neck edge 6 sts once, 3 (4, 4, 4) sts once, then 2 sts once. At the same time, work shoulder shaping by BO at each armhole edge 5 (6, 6, 6) sts once, then 5 (5, 5, 6) sts once, then 5 (5, 6, 6) sts once, then 5 (5, 5, 6) sts once, then 5 (6, 6, 6) sts once.

Front

Work same as back until armholes measure 5¾ (6¼, 6¾, 7¼)" (14.5 [16, 17, 18.5] cm), and end having just completed a RS row—91 (97, 103, 109) sts.

Shape front neck and shoulders: Cont in patt as established, work 38 (41, 42, 44) sts, BO center 15 (15, 19, 21) sts, join a separate ball of yarn, work in patt to end—38 (41, 42, 44) sts at each side. Working each side separately in patt, BO at each neck edge 3 (4, 4, 4) sts once, then 2 sts twice—31 (33, 34, 36) sts at each side. *Note:* The rest of the neck shaping and shoulder shaping are worked at the same time; read the next section through to the end before proceeding. Work fully fashioned decreases as follows every RS row 5 times, then every other RS row (every 4 rows) once: On first shoulder work to last 4 sts,

ssk, k2; on second shoulder k2, k2tog, work to end—6 sts decreased from each side of neck when all neck decreases have been completed. At the same time, when armholes measure 7½ (8, 8½, 9)" (19 [20.5, 21.5, 23] cm), work shoulder shaping as for back.

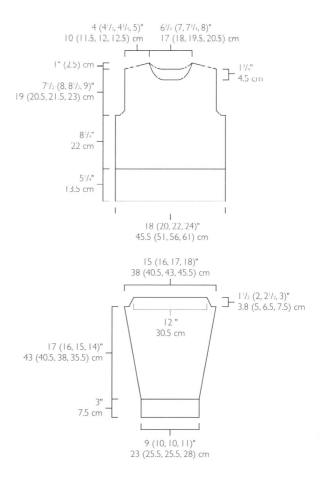

Sleeves

Lace trim: CO 55 (61, 61, 67) sts using long-tailed cast-on with beads as for back.

Reel off about 3 yd (3 m) of yarn, make a slipknot and place it on the ndl. Prestring about 18 (20, 20, 22) beads on the short tail strand. With tail yarn on thumb and working yarn on index finger, CO 1 st (2 sts on ndl). *BUB, CO3; rep from * until there are 53 (59, 59, 65) sts on ndl. BUB, CO 2 more sts—55 (61, 61, 67) sts total.

Work setup row without beads as follows: (WS) P2, knit to last 2 sts, end p2. Change to lace trim patt (Rows 1–8) from chart and repeat Rows 1–8 two more times, then work Rows 1–4 once more, inc 6 (0, 0, 6) sts evenly in last row—29 rows total, including the setup row; piece measures about 3" (7.5 cm) from beg; 61 (61, 61, 73) sts.

Change to Rows 9–12 as for back and front and repeat Rows 9–12 to end, working shaping as given below. *Note:* For sleeve shaping, work increased sts in St st until there are enough sts to work them into the patt; maintain at least 2 selvedge sts outside any yo/sk2p combinations or beaded sts as for back and front.

Beg with the next RS row, work fully fashioned increases as follows every 4 rows 0 (0, 4, 0) times, then every 6 rows 5 (18, 17, 18) times, then every 8 rows 10 (0, 0, 0) times: K2, M1 (see Abbreviations, page 146), work in patt to last 2 sts, M1, k2—91 (97, 103, 109) sts when all increases have been completed. Work even until piece measures 20 (19, 18, 17)" (51 [48.5, 45.5, 43] cm) from beg; end having just completed a WS row.

Shape sleeve cap: Cont in patt, maintaining at least 2 sts outside patt at each selvedge as before, BO 4 (4, 5, 6) sts at the beg of the next 2 rows—83 (89, 93, 97) sts. Dec 1 st fully fashioned at each side of the next 5 (8, 10, 12) RS rows as follows: K2, k2tog, work in patt to last 4 sts, ssk, k2—73 sts. Work 1 row on WS. BO all sts on next RS row.

Finishing

Weave in ends. Block pieces to measurements. Sew shoulder seams. Set sleeves in armholes. Sew sleeve and side seams.

Neckband

Using cir needle and RS facing, beg at right shoulder seam, pick up and knit 42 (45, 48, 51) sts across back neck, then pick up and knit 54 (57, 60, 63) sts evenly across front neck—96 (102, 108, 114) sts. Place marker to indicate beg of round (rnd). Working in the rnd with the RS of piece facing you at all times, work lace trim in the rnd as follows:

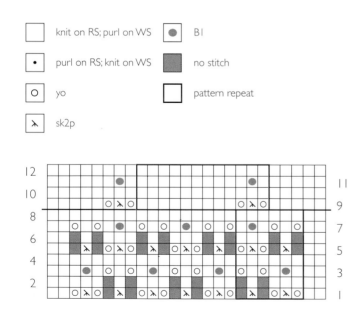

	knit on RS; purl on WS		BI
	purl on RS; knit on WS		no stitch
	yo		pattern repeat
	sk2p		

Rnd 1: *Yo, sk2p, yo, sk2p; rep from * around—64 (68, 72, 76) sts.

Rnd 2: Knit.

Rnd 3: *K1, place bead on next st and sl it purlwise wyib, k1, yo, k1, yo; rep from * around—96 (102, 108, 114) sts.

Rnd 4: Knit.

Rnd 5: *Sk2p, yo, sk2p, yo; rep from * around—64 (68, 72, 76) sts.

Rnd 6: Knit.

Rnd 7: *Yo, k1, yo, k1, place bead on next st and sl it purlwise wyib, k1; rep from * around—96 (102, 108, 114) sts.

Rnd 8: Knit.

After Rnd 8 has been completed, work Rnds 1–4 once more—12 rnds total; neckband measures about 1¼" (3.2 cm). On the next rnd, BO all sts loosely as if to knit. Weave in ends.

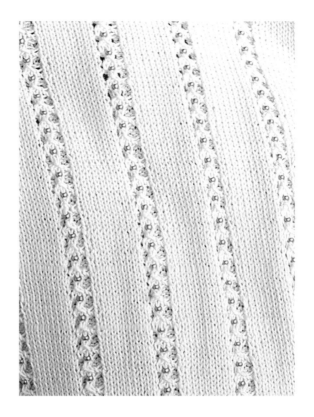

Bogus Bohus Cardigan

This cardigan features layers and layers of stitchery and beadwork that *look* intricate but really aren't. Slip-stitching means that you need to handle only one color at a time. When you add beads to form another pattern within the existing pattern, you also create another dimension of color and texture. I love getting a lot of bang for my buck. And I'll say it once again: This design looks difficult, but it's a lot easier to do than you first think.

Finished Size

38 (43, 47½, 52½)" (95.5 [109, 120.5, 133.5] cm) bust/chest circumference. Cardigan shown measures 43" (109 cm). This garment is intended to be loose fitting.

Materials

- Yarn: Brown Sheep Nature Spun Worsted (100% wool; 245 yd [224 m]/100 g): #N42 royal purple, #N81 cranberry fog, and #N94 Bev's bear (brown), 2 (2, 3, 3) skeins each.

- Beads: Size 3 or 5.5mm glass pebble beads: about 1,000. Shown in #05081 coal, from Mill Hill/Gay Bowles Sales.

- Needles: Size 7 (4.5 mm): straight and 29" (70-cm) circular (cir). Adjust needle size if necessary to obtain the correct gauge.

- Notions: Six ¾" (1.9 cm) buttons; steel crochet hook size 5 (1.75 mm) or smaller, or small bead hook; stitch markers; tapestry needle.

Gauge

20 sts and 26 rows = 4" (10 cm) in basket weave pattern; 20 sts and 30 rows = 4" (10 cm) in body slip-stitch pattern; 20 sts and 34 rows = 4" (10 cm) in yoke and neck slip-stitch patterns.

Special Notes

Slipped stitches are slipped as if to purl.

Do not cut the yarn at each color change. Instead, carry the colors not in use along the selvedges and catch them by laying the strands of the unused colors over the working strand before working the first stitch of the row. This step will lock the unused strands in the U-turn of the working yarn (see illustration at right).

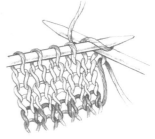

Catching the yarn not in use at the edge

Special Abbreviations

B1: Bead 1. Place bead on hook. Work to the stitch that will hold the bead, hook the top of the stitch, transfer the bead to the stitch by pushing it off the hook with your finger, and pull the top of the stitch up through the bead hole. Return the stitch to the left needle and knit it on RS, or purl it on WS.

Back

Basket weave trim: With purple, CO 95 (107, 119, 131) sts. Changing colors as indicated, work Rows 1–30 of basket weave and body slip-stitch chart, which are written out in words as follows:

Row 1: (RS) With purple, K1, *k3, p3; rep from * to last 4 sts, end k4.

Row 2: P1, *p3, k3; rep from * to last 4 sts, end p4.

Row 3: Rep Row 1.

Row 4: P1, *p1, B1 (see Special Abbreviations), p1, k3; rep from * to last 4 sts, end p1, B1, p2.

Rows 5 and 6: Rep Rows 1 and 2.

Row 7: Change to cranberry. K1, *p3, k3; rep from * to last 4 sts, end p3, k1.

Row 8: P1, *k3, p3; rep from * to last 4 sts, end k3, p1.

Row 9: Rep Row 7.

Row 10: P1, *k3, p1, B1, p1; rep from * to last 4 sts, end k3, p1.

Rows 11 and 12: Rep Rows 7 and 8.

Rows 13–18: Change to brown and rep Rows 1–6.

Rows 19–24: Change to cranberry and rep Rows 7–12.

Rows 25–30: Change to purple and rep Rows 1–6.

When 30 rows have been completed, piece measures about 4¾" (12 cm).

Body slip-stitch patt: Changing colors as indicated, work rows 31–46 of basket weave and body slip-stitch chart, and *at the same time* apply beads as follows: on Row 37, B1 at center on St 48 (54, 60, 66); on Row 41, B1 on St 45 (51, 57, 63), and St 51 (57, 63, 69); on Row 45, B1 on St 42 (48, 54, 60), St 48 (54, 60, 66), and St 54 (60, 66, 72). No beads are applied to Row 33 on the first rep of Rows 31–46.

Rows 31–46 are written out in words as foll; remember to work B1 on Rows 37, 41, and 45 as given for the chart instructions above:

Rows 31, 33, 39, and 41: (RS) K1, p4, *sl 1 with yarn in back (wyib), p5; rep from * to last 6 sts, end sl 1 wyib, p4, k1.

Rows 32, 34, 40, and 42: P1, k4, sl 1 with yarn in front (wyif), *k5, sl 1 wyif; rep from * to last 5 sts, end k5, p1.

Rows 35, 37, 43, and 45: K1, p1, *sl 1 wyib, p5; rep from * to last 3 sts, end sl 1 wyib, p1, k1.

Rows 36, 38, 44, and 46: P1, k1, *sl 1 wyif, k5; rep from * to last 3 sts, sl 1 wyif, k1, p1.

When Rows 31–46 have been completed, rep these rows three more times, and for these reps work B1 on Row 33 on St 45 (51, 57, 63) and St 51 (57, 63, 69), exactly as for Row 41—94 rows completed; piece measures about 13¼" (33.5 cm). With purple, work Rows 47–52 of basket weave and body slip-stitch chart once— 100 rows completed; piece measures about 14" (35.5 cm).

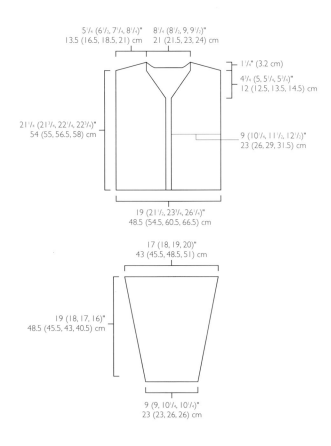

5¼ (6½, 7¼, 8¼)"
13.5 (16.5, 18.5, 21) cm

8¼ (8½, 9, 9½)"
21 (21.5, 23, 24) cm

1¼" (3.2 cm)

4¾ (5, 5¼, 5¾)"
12 (12.5, 13.5, 14.5) cm

21¼ (21¾, 22¼, 22¾)"
54 (55, 56.5, 58) cm

9 (10¼, 11½, 12½)"
23 (26, 29, 31.5) cm

19 (21½, 23¾, 26¼)"
48.5 (54.5, 60.5, 66.5) cm

17 (18, 19, 20)"
43 (45.5, 48.5, 51) cm

19 (18, 17, 16)"
48.5 (45.5, 43, 40.5) cm

9 (9, 10¼, 10¼)"
23 (23, 26, 26) cm

Legend

- knit on RS; purl on WS with color indicated
- · purl on RS; knit on WS with color indicated
- ● B1 with color indicated
- purple
- cranberry
- brown
- V sl 1 st as if to purl with yarn in back on RS; sl 1 as if to purl with yarn in front on WS
- pattern repeat

Basket Weave and Body Slip Stitch

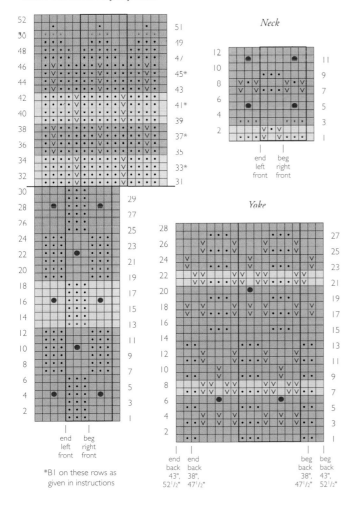

Neck

end left front   beg right front

Yoke

end left front   beg right front

end back 43", 38", 52½", 47½"   beg back 38", 43", 47½", 52½"

*B1 on these rows as given in instructions

Yoke slip-stitch patt: Work Rows 1–28 of yoke chart, beginning and ending where indicated for your size, and changing colors as shown. Rows 1–28 are written out in words as follows:

Row 1: (RS) With purple, k0 (1, 0, 1), p1 (2, 1, 2), *k5, p3; rep from * to last 6 (8, 6, 8) sts, end k5, p1 (2, 1, 2), k0 (1, 0, 1).

Row 2: Purl across.

Row 3: Change to cranberry, k0 (1, 0, 1), p1 (2, 1, 2), *[sl 1 wyib, k1] twice, sl 1 wyib, p3; rep from * to last 6 (8, 6, 8) sts, end [sl 1 wyib, k1] twice, sl 1 wyib, p1 (2, 1, 2), k0 (1, 0, 1).

Row 4: P1 (3, 1, 3), *[sl 1 wyif, p1] twice, sl 1 wyif, p3; rep from * , ending last rep as p1 (3, 1, 3).

Row 5: Change to purple, k0 (1, 0, 1), p1 (2, 1, 2), *k5, p3; rep from * to last 6 (8, 6, 8) sts, end k5, p1 (2, 1, 2), k0 (1, 0, 1).

Row 6: P3 (5, 3, 5), B1, *p7, B1; rep from * to last 3 (5, 3, 5) sts, end p3 (5, 3, 5).

Row 7: Change to brown, k0 (1, 0, 1), p1 (2, 1, 2), *sl 2 wyib, k1, sl 2 wyib, p3; rep from * to last 6 (8, 6, 8) sts, end sl 2 wyib, k1, sl 2 wyib, p1 (2, 1, 2), k0 (1, 0, 1).

Row 8: P1 (3, 1, 3), *sl 2 wyif, p1, sl 2 wyif, p3; rep from *, ending last rep p1 (3, 1, 3).

Row 9: Change to purple, k0 (1, 0, 1), p1 (2, 1, 2), *k2, sl 1 wyib, k2, p3; rep from * to last 6 (8, 6, 8) sts, end k2, sl 1 wyib, k2, p1 (2, 1, 2), k0 (1, 0, 1).

Row 10: P3 (5, 3, 5), *sl 1 wyif, p7; rep from * to last 4 (6, 4, 6) sts, end sl 1 wyif, p3 (5, 3, 5).

Row 11: Change to cranberry, k0 (1, 0, 1), p1 (2, 1, 2), *sl 1 wyib, k3, sl 1 wyib, p3; rep from * to last 6 (8, 6, 8) sts, end sl 1 wyib, k3, sl 1 wyib, p1 (2, 1, 2), k0 (1, 0, 1).

Row 12: *P3, sl 1 wyif; rep from * to last 3 sts, end p3.

Row 13: Change to purple, k0 (1, 0, 1), p1 (2, 1, 2), *k5, p3; rep from * to last 6 (8, 6, 8) sts, end k5, p1 (2, 1, 2), k0 (1, 0, 1).

Row 14: Purl across.

Row 15: K2 (4, 2, 4), *p3, k5; rep from * to last 5 (7, 5, 7) sts, end p3, k2 (4, 2, 4).

Row 16: Purl across.

Row 17: Change to cranberry, k0 (1, 0, 1), sl 0 (1, 0, 1) wyib, k1, *sl 1 wyib, p3, [sl 1 wyib, k1] twice; rep from *, ending last rep [sl 1 wyib, k1] once (twice, once, twice).

Row 18: [P1, sl 1 wyif] once (twice, once, twice), *p3, [sl 1 wyif, p1] twice, sl 1 wyif; rep from * to last 5 (7, 5, 7) sts, end p3, [sl 1 wyif, p1] once (twice, once, twice).

Row 19: Change to purple, k2 (4, 2, 4), *p3, k5; rep from * to last 5 (7, 5, 7) sts, end p3, k2 (4, 2, 4).

Row 20: P7 (9, 7, 9), *B1, p7; rep from *, ending last rep p7 (9, 7, 9).

Row 21: Change to brown, k1 (2, 1, 2), sl 0 (1, 0, 1) wyib, *sl 1 wyib, p3, sl 2 wyib, k1, sl 1 wyib; rep from * to last 6 (8, 6, 8) sts, end sl 1 wyib, p3, k2 (0, 2, 0), sl 0 (2, 0, 2) wyib, k0 (2, 0, 2).

Row 22: P2, sl 0 (2, 0, 2) wyif, *p3, sl 2 wyif, p1, sl 2 wyif; rep from * to last 5 (7, 5, 7) sts, end p3, sl 1 (2, 1, 2) wyif, p1 (2, 1, 2).

Row 23: Change to purple, k0 (1, 0, 1), sl 0 (1, 0, 1) wyib, k2, *p3, k2, sl 1 wyib, k2; rep from * to last 5 (7, 5, 7) sts, end p3, k2, sl 0 (1, 0, 1) wyib, k0 (1, 0, 1).

Row 24: P0 (1, 0, 1), sl 0 (1, 0, 1) wyif, p7, *sl 1 wyif, p7; rep from * to last 0 (2, 0, 2) sts, end sl 0 (1, 0, 1) wyif, p0 (1, 0, 1).

Row 25: Change to cranberry, k1 (3, 1, 3), *sl 1 wyib, p3, sl 1 wyib, k3; rep from *, ending last rep k1 (3, 1, 3).

Row 26: P1 (3, 1, 3), *sl 1 wyif, p3; rep from *, ending last rep p1 (3, 1, 3).

Row 27: Change to purple, k2 (4, 2, 4), *p3, k5; rep from * to last 5 (7, 5, 7) sts, end p3, k2 (4, 2, 4).

Row 28: Purl across.

When Rows 1–28 have been completed, work Rows 1–12 once more; 40 rows total of yoke chart; piece measures about 18¾" (47.5 cm). With cranberry, work 4 rows St st.

Neck slip-stitch patt: Work Rows 1–12 of neck chart, changing colors as shown. Rows 1–12 are written out in words as follows:

Row 1: (RS) Change to brown, k1, *p3, sl 1 wyib, k1, sl 1 wyib; rep from * to last 4 sts, end p3, k1.

Row 2: P4, *sl 1 wyif, k1, sl 1 wyif, p3; rep from * to last st, end p1.

Row 3: Change to cranberry, k1, *p3, k3; rep from * to last 4 sts, end p3, k1.

Row 4: Purl across.

Row 5: K2, *B1, k5; rep from * to last 3 sts, end B1, k2.

Row 6: Purl across.

Row 7: Change to purple, k1, *sl 1 wyib, k1, sl 1 wyib, p3; rep from * to last 4 sts, end [sl 1 wyib, k1] twice.

Row 8: P1, sl 1 wyif, k1, sl 1 wyif, *p3, sl 1 wyif, k1, sl 1 wyif; rep from * to last st, end p1.

Row 9: Change to cranberry, k4, *p3, k3; rep from * to last st, end k1.

Row 10: Purl across.

Row 11: Rep Row 5.

Row 12: Purl across.

Rep Rows 1–12, until piece measures 21¼ (21¾, 22¼, 22¾)" (54 [55, 56.5, 58] cm) from beg, and end having just completed a WS row.

Shape shoulders and back neck: When shaping, if there are fewer than 2 sts between a bead and the selvedge, omit the bead. Cont in neck patt, BO 4 (5, 6, 7) sts at beg of next 2 rows—87 (97, 107, 117) sts rem. Mark center 25 (25, 27, 29) sts for center back neck. On the next row (RS), BO 4 (5, 6, 7) sts, work to marked center sts, join second ball of yarn, BO center 25 (25, 27, 29) sts, work to end. BO 4 (5, 6, 7) sts at beg of first section on next row; work second section even to end—27 (31, 34, 37) sts at each side. Working both sides separately, BO at each neck edge 3 (4, 4, 4) sts once, then 2 sts twice, then 1 st once, and *at the same time,* BO at each shoulder 4 (5, 6, 7) sts, then 5 (5, 6, 7) sts, then 5 (6, 6, 7) sts, then 5 (6, 7, 7) sts.

Left Front

Basket weave trim: With purple, CO 45 (51, 57, 63) sts. Work Row 1 of basket weave and body slip-stitch chart over first 43 (49, 55, 61) sts, ending where indicated, then work last 2 sts as k2 for center front edge. Keeping 2 sts in St st at center front edge throughout, work Rows 2–30 of basket weave and body chart.

Body slip-stitch patt: For Rows 31–46, the last pattern st worked before the St sts at center front will be St 2 of the patt rep. Work rows 31–46 of basket weave and body slip-stitch chart as for back, and *at the same time,* apply beads as follows: on Row 37, B1 on St 24 (30, 30, 36); on Row 41, B1 on St 21 (27, 27, 33), and St 27 (33, 33, 39); on Row 45, B1 on St 18 (24, 24, 30), St 24 (30, 30, 36), and St 30 (36, 36, 42). No beads are applied to Row 33 on the first rep of Rows 31–46.

When Rows 31–46 have been completed, rep these rows three more times, and for these reps work B1 on Row 33 on St 21 (27, 27, 33) and St 27 (33, 33, 39), exactly as for Row 41. With purple, work Rows 47–52 of basket weave and body slip-stitch chart once.

Yoke slip-stitch patt: Work Rows 1–28 of yoke chart, then work Rows 1–12 once more. *Note:* Beg the patt as indicated for your size, as for back; the last pattern st worked before the St sts at center front will be St 2 (6, 6, 2) of the patt repeat box. *At the same time,* when piece measures 16½ (16¾, 17, 17)" (42 [42.5, 43, 43] cm), end having just completed a WS row and begin front neck shaping.

Shape front neck: In shaping, if there are fewer than 2 sts between a bead and the selvedge, omit the bead. Beg decs as described below in yoke patt, and when all 40 rows of yoke patt have been completed, work 4 rows St st with cranberry, then change to neck patt as for back. Work fully fashioned dec on the next RS row as foll: Work in patt to last 3 sts, k2tog, k1—1 st dec'd. Work dec row every other row a total of 16 (17, 18, 19) times, then every 4 rows 2 times—27 (32, 37, 42) sts. Work even if necessary until piece measures 21¼ (21¾, 22¼, 22¾)" (54 [55, 56.5, 58] cm) from beg, and end having just completed a WS row.

Shape shoulders: BO at beg of RS rows 4 (5, 6, 7) sts three times, then 5 (5, 6, 7) sts once, then 5 (6, 6, 7) sts once, then 5 (6, 7, 7) sts once.

Right Front

Basket weave trim: With purple, CO 45 (51, 57, 63) sts. Next row: K2 for center front edge, work Row 1 of basket weave and body slip-stitch chart over 43 (49, 55, 61) sts, beginning where indicated. Keeping 2 sts in St st at center front edge throughout, work Rows 2–30 of basket weave and body chart.

Body slipstitch patt: For Rows 31–42, the patt begins with St 5 of chart (1 st before the repeat box). Work rows 31–46 of basket weave and body slip-stitch chart as for back, and *at the same time,* apply beads as for left front, beginning by placing the single bead of Row 37 on St 22 (22, 28, 28), and placing rem beads in the same relative positions as on left front. No beads are applied to Row 33 on the first rep of Rows 31–46.

When Rows 31–46 have been completed, rep these rows three more times, and for these reps work B1 on Row 33, exactly as for Row 41. With purple, work Rows 47–52 of basket weave and body slip-stitch chart once.

Yoke slip-stitch patt: Work Rows 1–28 of yoke chart, then work Row 1–12 once more. *Note:* Set up patt by working 2 selvedge sts at center front, beg the patt with St 4 (8, 8, 4) of the repeat box, and end where indicated for your size, as for back. *At the same time,* when piece measures 16½ (16¾, 17, 17)" (42 [42.5, 43, 43] cm), end having just completed a WS row and begin front neck shaping.

Shape front neck: In shaping, if there are fewer than 2 sts between a bead and the selvedge, omit the bead. Beg decs as described below in yoke patt, and when all 40 rows of yoke patt have been completed, work 4 rows St st with cranberry, then change to neck patt as for back. Work fully fashioned dec on the next RS row as foll: K1, ssk, work in patt to end—1 st dec'd. Work dec row every other row a total of 16 (17, 18, 19) times, then every 4 rows 2 times—27 (32, 37, 42) sts. Work even if necessary until piece measures 21¼ (21¾, 22¼, 22¾)" (54 [55, 56.5, 58] cm) from beg and end having just completed a RS row.

Shape shoulders: BO at beg of WS rows 4 (5, 6, 7) sts three times, then 5 (5, 6, 7) sts once, then 5 (6, 6, 7) sts once, then 5 (6, 7, 7) sts once.

Sleeves

With purple, CO 45 (45, 51, 51) sts. Establish basket weave patt from Row 1 of chart as foll: K2 (edge sts, keep in St st throughout) work in patt over center 41 (41, 47, 47) sts, k2 (edge sts, keep in St st throughout). In shaping, if there are fewer than 2 sts between a bead and the selvedge, omit the bead. Work in basket weave patt (Rows 1–30 only), and beg on Row 5 (5, 5, 3), inc 1 st at each side inside the edge sts, every 4 rows 4 (16, 16, 25) times, then every 6 rows 16 (7, 6, 0) times, working new sts into patt—85 (91, 95, 101) sts. Work even in basket weave patt until piece measures about 19 (18, 17, 16)" (48.5 [45.5, 43, 40.5] cm) and end having just completed a 6-row stripe. BO all sts.

Finishing

Weave in ends. Block pieces to measurements. Sew shoulder seams. Measure down 8½ (9, 9½, 10)" (21.5 [23, 24, 25.5] cm) from shoulder seams along each side of back and each front and place markers. Sew top of sleeves between markers. Sew sleeve and side seams.

Front Band

Using cir needle and brown, with RS facing and beg at lower right front opening, pick up and knit 69 sts from bottom edge to beg of V-neck shaping, mark last st, pick up and knit 107 (113, 119, 125) sts to beg of left V-neck shaping, mark the next st picked up and knit 69 sts from left V-neck shaping to lower edge of left front—245 (251, 257, 263) sts. Work front band back and forth on cir needle as foll:

Row 1: (WS) Sl 1 wyif, *p3, k3; rep from * to last 4 sts, p3, sl 1 wyif.

Row 2: (RS) K1, working sts as they appear, work to marked st, [k1, yo, k1] all in marked st, work in patt to second marked st, [k1, yo, k1] all in marked st, work in patt to end—249 (255, 261, 267) sts.

Row 3: Sl 1 wyif, work in patt to 1 st before marked st, p3 (worked over the k1, yo, k1 of previous row), work in patt to 1 st before next marked st, p3 (worked over the k1, yo, k1 of previous row), work sts in patt to last st, sl 1 wyif.

Row 4: (Buttonhole row) K1, *work 9 sts in patt, p1, p2tog, yo for buttonhole; rep from * 4 more times (5 buttonholes completed), work in patt to marked st, [k1, yo twice, k1] all in marked st, work to next marked st, [k1, yo, k1] all in marked st, work in patt to end.

Row 5: Sl 1 wyif, work in patt to 1 st before first marked st, p1, k1, p1, work in patt to 1 st before next marked st, p1, k1, drop extra yo wrap, p1, work in patt to end—253 (259, 265, 271) sts.

Row 6: Work in patt to buttonhole, *purl into yo eyelet of 2 rows below to enlarge the buttonhole and drop the st on the needle above it, work in patt to next buttonhole; rep from * until you arrive at first marked st, [p1, yo, p1] all in yo eyelet 2 rows below, work in patt to next marked st, [p1, yo, p1] all in marked st, work in patt to end, hooking shanked buttons onto sts on left front to correspond to buttonhole positions if desired (optional)—257 (263, 269, 275) sts.

Row 7: Sl 1 wyif, work in patt to first marked st, work k3 over [p1, yo, p1] of previous row, work in patt to next marked st, work k3 over [p1, yo, p1] of previous row, work in patt to end.

Row 8: BO all sts in patt.

Weave in ends. Sew buttons to left front to correspond to buttonholes if they were not hooked on in Row 6.

CHAPTER 7

Separate Strand of Yarn with Beads

Mosaic Madness Bag

Beads with small holes can actually be applied to knitting without sewing. Even if the bead hole is too small to accommodate yarn, some kind of thread will be able to go through the bead.

The key here is to get a coordinating thread that is the same color as the yarn. Place the beads on the thread and knit the yarn and thread together, very much like a run-along, mixer-type yarn. I find nylon thread durable and strong, and it comes in a multitude of colors. Silk also works well but is costly. But never fear; even thin, high-twist cotton will do the job. You may also use bigger beads since this method has little overall effect on the gauge of the stitches.

Prestring the beads on the matching thread. Knit the thread, held together with the yarn, until a bead is desired. At this point, *separate* the beaded thread from the yarn and bring it to the right side. Work the stitch(es) behind the bead, with just the knitting yarn. Return the beaded thread to where the knitting yarn is and continue to work them both together until the next bead placement.

In a way, this technique is similar to the slipped-stitch method of Chapter 3. The difference here is that any stitches behind the beads are knitted, not slipped, and the beads sit on a float of carry-along thread, not the knitting yarn. Thus, longer beads (or multiple beads) may be used within reason. Too long a float will catch on things, snag, and elongate. However, the thread, being knitted along with the yarn, is well anchored, and will not move around too much. Thus, stretching and sagging should not pose much of a problem.

Run-along thread with beads knitted together with yarn

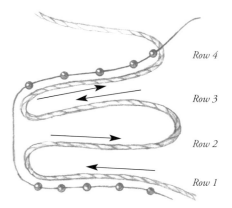

Row 4

Row 3

Row 2

Row 1

Potential beading rows

Use any stitch pattern. You can create an interesting effect if you contrast the thread and yarn colors. Beads need not appear on every row. If you're working back and forth in flat knitting, however, there must be an even number of rows between beading rows. That is, if a right side row is worked as a beading row, the beaded thread is at the left-hand end of the knitting. A wrong side and another right-side row (or several wrong- and right-side rows) must be worked in order to get back to where the beaded thread is. The next beading row is then a wrong-side row. Of course, when you're working circularly or in the round, as in the Mosaic Madness Bag, this is a moot point. One may bead on *any* row in this instance.

One does not even need to bead across a whole row. Take a look at the illustration below to see how the beaded thread can go upward on a diagonal. Knit the beaded thread together with the yarn, on both the stitch before and after where the bead appears. Doing so will secure the bead in place.

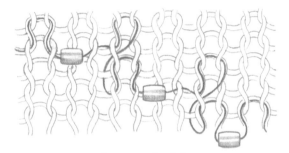

Beads not across the whole row

Mosaic Madness Bag

A mixed mélange of color and texture, this bag uses beads with holes too small to normally knit on yarn. The beads are also rather large in size, again not the type normally used with "regular" beaded knitting. The secret is in the carry-along thread. And note how the bottom shaping expands the bag to make it very functional.

Finished Size
About 12" (30.5 cm) wide and 7½" (19 cm) high, not including handles.

Materials
- Yarn: Aurora Garnstudio Cotton Viscose (54% cotton, 46% viscose; 120 yd [110 m]/50 g): #04 gold, #10 olive, and #06 rust, 1 skein each.

- Beads: Glass rectangular beads, about 6mm square in cross section and 2cm long: about 144. Beads shown from Beads World, style number not available. Size 8mm round onakite beads: about 40. Beads shown from Threads, style number not available. Size 6mm faceted fire-polished beads: about 132. Shown in #132 smoke topaz, from Threads.

- Needles: Size 3 (3.25 mm): set of five double-pointed (dpn), 10" (25.5 cm) long preferred, but no less than 8" (20.5 cm) long. Adjust needle size if necessary to obtain the correct gauge.

- Notions: Beading needle; one 100-yd (100-m) spool of nylon thread in each of three colors to match yarn (shown: Nymo size B in gold, olive, and rust from Beads World); stitch markers; two D-shaped bamboo handles (shown: from Beads World); tapestry needle.

Gauge
28 sts and 32 rows = 4" (10 cm) in St st.

Special Notes
Prestring beads on nylon thread before working. Glass rectangles go on olive thread, onakite goes on rust, and topaz goes on gold.

Slipped sts are slipped as if to purl with yarn in back.

Work with one strand of yarn held together with one strand of matching beaded thread, unless otherwise noted.

Special Abbreviations
BSTF: Beaded Strand to Front. Separate beaded strand and yarn and bring beaded strand to front of work.

BSTB: Beaded Strand to Back. Bring beaded strand to back of work and resume working with both beaded strand and yarn held together.

Bobble
Row 1: [K1, yo, k1, yo, k1] all in same st—5 sts made from 1 st. Turn, sl 1, k4; turn, sl 1, p4; turn, sl 1, k4; turn sl 1, p2tog twice, pass each of the first 2 sts over the last st to dec back to 1 st.

Base
Using a pair of dpn, make a slipknot with one strand of olive yarn and place it on the needle.
Row 1: (RS) [K1, yo, k1] all in slipknot—3 sts.

Row 2 and All WS Rows: Purl across.

Row 3: K1, [k1, yo, k1] all in center st, k1—5 sts.

Row 5: K2, [k1, yo, k1] all in center st, k2—7 sts.

Row 7: K3, [k1, yo, k1] all in center st, k3—9 sts.

Work even in St st on 9 sts until 98 rows total have been completed—piece measures about 12¼" (31 cm) from beg.

Row 99: K3, sl 1, k2tog, pass slipped st over (psso), k3—7 sts.

Row 101: K2, sl 1, k2tog, psso, k2—5 sts.

Row 103: K1, sl 1, k2tog, psso, k1—3 sts.

Row 105: Sl 1, k2tog, psso—1 st. Do not cut yarn.

Body

Mark the rem st for the beg of the round (rnd). With RS facing, pick up and knit 90 sts evenly along one selvedge of base and distribute these sts evenly on 2 dpn; with a third dpn, pick up and knit 1 st in the beg slipknot and mark this st; pick up and knit 90 sts evenly along other selvedge of base and distribute these sts evenly on 2 dpn—182 sts. The body of the bag is worked in the rnd with RS facing you at all times.

Beg patt from chart, working Rnds 1 and 2 with yarn only. On Rnd 3, join matching beaded strand and cont in patt from chart until Rnd 68 has been completed. Rnds 1–68 are written out in words as follows:

Rnd 1: With olive yarn only, knit.

Rnd 2: With olive yarn only, sl 1, knit to first marked st, sl 1, knit to end.

Rnds 3 and 4: Join matching beaded strand and rep Rnds 1 and 2.

Rnd 5: *K1, [k2, BSTF, k2, BSTB] 22 times, k2; rep from * for other side of bag.

Rnd 6: With olive yarn only, sl 1, knit to marked st, sl 1, knit to end.

Rnd 7: With olive yarn only, knit.

Rnd 8: Join matching beaded strand, sl 1, knit to marked st, sl 1, knit to end.

Rnd 9: *K2, [k2, BSTF, k2, BSTB] 22 times, k1; rep from * for other side of bag.

Rnds 10, 11, and 12: Rep Rnds 6, 7, and 8.

Rnd 13: *K1, [BSTF, k2, BSTB, k2] 22 times, BSTF, k2, BSTB; rep from * for other side of bag. Cut beaded strand.

Rnds 14–17: Rep Rnds 6 and 7 twice.

Rnd 18: Join rust yarn, *sl 1, [k2 olive, k2 rust] 22 times, k2 olive; rep from * for other side of bag.

Rnd 19: *K1 olive, [k2 olive, p2 rust] 22 times, k2 olive; rep from * for other side of bag.

Rnds 20 and 21: Rep Rnds 6 and 7.

Rnd 22: *Sl 1, k1 rust, [k2 olive, k2 rust] 22 times, k1 olive; rep from * for other side of bag.

Rnd 23: *K1 olive, p1 rust, [k2 olive, p2 rust] 22 times, k1 olive; rep from * for other side of bag.

Rnds 24 and 25: Rep Rnds 6 and 7.

Rnd 26: *Sl 1, [k2 rust, k2 olive] 22 times, k2 rust; rep from * for other side of bag.

Rnd 27: *K1 olive, [p2 rust, k2 olive] 22 times, p2 rust; rep from * for other side of bag.

Rnds 28 and 29: Rep Rnds 6 and 7.

Rnd 30: *Sl 1, k1 olive, [k2 rust, k2 olive] 22 times, k1 rust; rep from * for other side of bag.

Rnd 31: *K2 olive, [p2 rust, k2 olive] 22 times, p1 rust; rep from * for other side of bag. Cut olive yarn.

Rnds 32, 33, and 34: With rust, rep Rnds 6 and 7, then work Rnd 6 once more.

Body

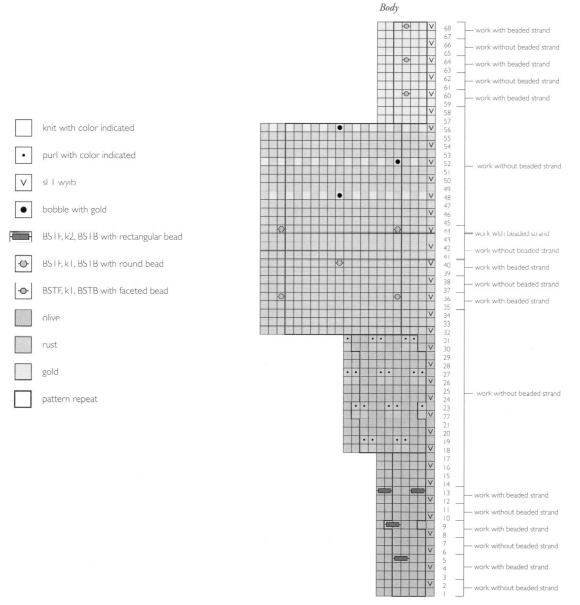

knit with color indicated

purl with color indicated

sl 1 wyib

bobble with gold

BSTF, k2, BSTB with rectangular bead

BSTF, k1, BSTB with round bead

BSTF, k1, BSTB with faceted bead

olive

rust

gold

pattern repeat

Work chart once for first side of bag,
then begin chart again for second side of bag.

Rnd 35: Join matching beaded strand, knit.

Rnd 36: *Sl 1, k3, [BSTF, k1, BSTB, k13] 6 times, BSTF, k1, BSTB, k2; rep from * for other side of bag.

Rnds 37 and 38: With rust, work Rnd 7, then work Rnd 6.

Rnd 39: Rep Rnd 35.

Rnd 40: *Sl 1, k3, [k7, BSTF, k1, BSTB, k6] 6 times, k3; rep from * for other side of bag.

Rnds 41, 42, and 43: Rep Rnds 33, 34, and 35.

Rnd 44: Rep Rnd 36. Cut beaded strand.

Rnds 45, 46, and 47: With rust, rep Rnd 7, then work Rnds 6 and 7 once.

Rnd 48: Join gold. *Sl 1, k1 gold, k1 rust, k1 gold, **[k1 rust, k1 gold] 3 times, k1 rust, bobble gold, [k1 rust, k1 gold] 3 times; rep from ** 5 more times, then rep entire sequence from * for other side of bag.

Rnds 49, 50, and 51: With rust, work Rnd 7, then rep Rnds 6 and 7 once.

Rnd 52: *Sl 1, k1 rust, k1 gold, k1 rust, **bobble gold, [k1 rust, k1 gold] 6 times, k1 rust; rep from ** 5 more times, then rep entire sequence from * for other side of bag.

Rnds 53, 54, and 55: With rust, work Rnd 7, then rep Rnds 6 and 7 once.

Rnd 56: Rep Rnd 48. Cut rust yarn.

Rnds 57 and 58: With gold, work Rnd 6, then Rnd 7.

Rnd 59: Join matching beaded strand, knit.

Rnd 60: *Sl 1, [k2, BSTF, k1, BSTB, k1] 22 times, k2; rep from * for other side of bag.

Rnds 61–68: Rep Rnds 57–60 twice. Cut beaded strand.

With gold, work k1, p1 rib all the way around for 4 rnds.

Handle Extensions

BO first 30 sts in k1, p1 rib, work in rib patt until there are 31 sts on right needle, join second ball of yarn, BO next 60 sts, work in rib patt until there are 31 sts in the next group on right needle, BO 30 sts—two groups of 31 sts rem. Working each group separately, work in rib patt as established for 16 rows. BO all sts.

Finishing

Weave in ends. Wrap handle extension around straight side of D-shaped handle, and sew to WS. Rep for other handle.

Sewing on Beads
Raj Pillow

Sewing beads onto a knitted fabric after the knitting is completed is the most spontaneous and versatile method, yet not very "knitterly" or crochet-like. Not an integral part of the fabric, the beading is "plastered" on afterwards. Yet the advantages are many. There is no ripping out of the knitting or crocheting if you've made a mistake. There is very little planning involved before knitting or crocheting. Small beads with small holes are possible. Textured yarns such as chenille, bouclé, slubbed and nubbies, thick-and-thins, and so forth can be used as the base.

However, there are also disadvantages. Sewing thread has no stretch or give. Use it on stretch knits and watch the threads snap and break, cascading the beads to the floor. The threads can also render some of the knit fabric unstretchable, which results in puckering in places.

To alleviate some of these concerns, use strong, sturdy thread. I find silky nylon ideal for its slight springiness and strength. In the early days of my knitting career, I thought I was so smart because I'd sewn beads on with elastic thread. I forgot about elastic's shelf life. That is, over time, elastic loses its elasticity. I had a sweater with loopy beads hanging down!

The finer the knitting or crocheting, the better the detail. Chunky knits and crochets do not offer as many stitch possibilities for bead placement. You can split the yarn by inserting the beading needle through the middle of the strand. However, I worry about the yarn weakening over time with this method, and sewing on beads gets around this problem.

If you make clusters of beads close together, there is no need to break off the sewing thread with each bead. Start off by securing the bead with a knot in a spot where a bead is to be placed. Then, after sewing the bead in place, knot off the thread again in the same spot.

Some knitters/crocheters are able to eyeball the beadwork and work free-form. If you are not comfortable with this spontaneous approach, sketch out the beadwork on tissue, lay it over the project, and pin it down or baste it. Use the tissue as your template. After sewing the beads on, just tear away the tissue paper. This is how I beaded the Raj Pillow, worked in textured chenille.

Raj Pillow

The lush chenille is a marvelously textured backdrop for sewn beads. Since beads do not slide easily on this yarn and because the bead holes here are particularly small, sewing is a satisfying solution. You can make a crocheted pillow in a similar manner using chenille or other heavily textured novelty yarns.

Finished Size
About 12" (30.5 cm) square.

Materials
- Yarn: Crystal Palace Cotton Chenille (100% cotton; 98 yd [90 m]/50 g): #6320 sage, 3 skeins.

- Beads: Size 8 seed beads: about 100 gold and 75 off-white. Shown in #39 champagne and #343 pearl, from Toho Shoji. Size 4 bugle beads: about 325. Shown in #136 champagne, from Beads World.

- Needles: Size 7 (4.5 mm): straight. Adjust needle size if necessary to obtain the correct gauge.

- Notions: Beading needle; 100-yd (100-m) spool of nylon thread to match pillow or bead color (shown: Nymo size B in gold, from Beads World); crochet hook size G (4.5 mm); tapestry needle; 12" (30.5 cm) square pillow form or polyester fiberfill stuffing.

Gauge
16 sts and 32 rows = 4" (10 cm) in seed st.

Pillow Back and Front
CO 48 sts. Work all rows in seed st as follows:
Row 1: *K1, p1; rep from * to end.
Row 2: *P1, k1; rep from * to end.

Repeat Rows 1 and 2 until piece measures 12" (30.5 cm) from beg. BO all sts. Make a second piece the same as the first. Work 1 row of single crochet (sc) evenly around all 4 sides of each piece, turning the corners by working 3 sc into each corner.

Embroidery
Using the diagram as a guide, embellish one piece with beads. Beg with the pearl centers of each floral motif and work each flower out from the middle. Add the connecting lines of bugle beads, and "chicken-feet" clusters, then place four small flower motifs near the corners as shown.

Finishing
Weave in ends. With the right sides of the pillow pieces held together (wrong sides will be facing out), slip-stitch crochet around 3 sides of the pillow. Turn pillow right side out. Insert pillow form or stuffing. Slip-stitch crochet the last side closed.

CHAPTER 9

Crocheting on Beads, or Tambour Embroidery
Homage to Haring Jacket

Tambour embroidery is another method of affixing beads—after the fact—to any knitted or crocheted fabric. I use a crochet hook in lieu of a traditional tambour hook (which is very fine and sharp) because we are not placing beads on woven sewing fabrics. A latch hook, such as the kind used for rugs, is another tool alternative.

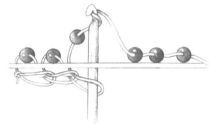

Hooking pre-beaded strand through fabric

The hook is on the back, or the wrong side, of the fabric. The yarn, prestrung with beads, is in the front, or the right side, of the fabric. To start off, make a slipknot on the prestrung yarn and bring the slipknot to the back, or wrong side, of the fabric and place onto hook. * Insert hook from back to front, or from wrong side to right side, and snuggle up a bead close to the fabric. Hook the yarn beyond the bead to the back, and bring the yarn through the loop already on the hook to form a slip-stitch chain in the back, or wrong side. Repeat from *. To end, snip yarn in front, bring it through the last loop on the back, and fasten.

While not necessary, it is easier to make one long, continuous line of beads. Doing so prevents frequent stopping and starting (which also requires you to weave in more ends later). The drawback is that a lot of beads need to be prestrung on the yarn, and that translates into a lot of shoving down.

This method is speedy, and mistakes can be easily ripped out by pulling the chain. Use the method atop heavily textured knits or crochets. However, the beaded strand should be smooth but not necessarily of the same weight as the knitting or crocheting yarn. It can also be in a color that contrasts with the knitting/crocheting yarn. Furthermore, beads need not appear behind each chain. You can make the beading sparser by doing a few extra chains before placing another bead up close to the work.

As with sewing on beads, you can sketch out the beading composition on tissue paper as a guide. Affix it to the project, either with pins or by basting. Tear away the tissue paper upon completion.

Homage to Haring Jacket

Here is a luscious chenille backdrop for applying beads once the garment has been knitted or crocheted. Beads do not slide on this yarn easily, and the holes are too small for such a thick yarn anyway. The yarn used for the tambour embroidery/ crochet can contrast with or match the jacket in both color and texture. Feel free to make a crocheted jacket in a similar manner and/or to use other heavily textured novelty yarns.

Finished Size

40 (44, 48, 52)" (101.5 [112, 122, 132] cm) bust/chest circumference. Jacket shown measures 44" (112 cm). This garment is intended to be loose fitting.

Materials

- Yarn: Lion Brand Chenille Thick & Quick (91% acrylic, 9% rayon; 100 yd [90 m]/weight varies, about 6 oz [170 g]): #146 dark purple, 4 (4, 5, 5) skeins. Lion Brand Glitterspun (60% acrylic, 27% cupro, 13% polyester; 115 yd [105 m]/50 g): #170 gold metallic, 1 (1, 2, 2) skeins.

- Beads: Size 3 or 5.5mm glass pebble beads: about 800. Shown in #05555 pink, from Mill Hill/Gay Bowles Sales.

- Needles: Size 11 (8 mm): 29" (70-cm) circular (cir). Adjust needle size if necessary to obtain the correct gauge.

- Notions: Bead-stringing needle; crochet hooks size I (5.5 mm) and L (8 mm); stitch holders; tapestry needle.

Gauge

8 sts and 14 rows = 4" (10 cm) in St st.

Special Notes

All pieces are worked flat, back and forth. The circular needle is used to accommodate the number and size of the stitches; it is not used for working in the round.

The body of the jacket is worked in one piece to the armholes, then divided for working the back and two fronts separately.

Prestring beads on metallic yarn before applying tambour embroidery; use about 200 beads per sleeve and 400 beads total for the back and fronts.

Lower Body

With chenille, CO 80 (88, 96, 104) sts. Work in St st until piece measures 12" (30.5 cm), ending with a WS row.

Divide for armholes: Work 19 (21, 23, 25) sts for right front, BO next 2 sts for armhole, work until there are 38 (42, 46, 50) sts on right needle for back, BO next 2 sts for armhole, work to end—19 (21, 23, 25) sts for each front, 38 (42, 46, 50) sts for back. Place front sts on holders.

Back

Rejoin yarn to back sts with WS facing and purl 1 row on WS. Cont in St st, shaping armholes by dec 1 st at each side every RS row 2 (3, 4, 5) times as follows: K1,

ssk, knit to last 3 sts, k2tog, k1—34 (36, 38, 40) sts rem when all decs have been completed. Work even in St st until armholes measure 8½ (9, 9½, 10)" (21.5 [23, 24, 25.5] cm). BO all sts.

Left Front

Return 19 (21, 23, 25) sts for left front to needle, join yarn with WS facing, and purl 1 row on WS. Cont in St st, shaping armholes by dec 1 st at beg of every RS row 2 (3, 4, 5) times as follows: K1, ssk, knit to end—17 (18, 19, 20) sts rem when all decs have been completed. Work even in St st until armholes measure 5½ (6, 6½, 7)" (14 [15, 16.5, 18] cm), ending with a RS row. At beg of next WS row, BO 3 (4, 4, 5) sts, work to end—14 (14, 15, 15) sts. Dec 1 st at the end of the next 4 RS rows as follows: Knit to last 3 sts, k2tog, k1—10 (10, 11, 11) sts rem when all decs have been completed. Work even until armholes measure 8½ (9, 9½, 10)" (21.5 [23, 24, 25.5] cm). BO all sts.

Right Front

Return 19 (21, 23, 25) sts for right front to needle, join yarn with WS facing, and purl 1 row on WS. Cont in St st, shaping armholes by dec 1 st at end of every RS row 2 (3, 4, 5) times as follows: Knit to last 3 sts, k2tog, k1—17 (18, 19, 20) sts rem when all decs have been completed. Work even in St st until armholes measure 5½ (6, 6½, 7)" (14 [15, 16.5, 18] cm), ending with a WS row. At beg of next RS row, BO 3 (4, 4, 5) sts, work to end—14 (14, 15, 15) sts. Dec 1 st at the beg of the next 4 RS rows as follows: K1, ssk, knit to end—10 (10, 11, 11) sts rem when all decs have been completed. Work even until armholes measure 8½ (9, 9½, 10)" (21.5 [23, 24, 25.5] cm). BO all sts.

Sleeves

With chenille, CO 18 (20, 20, 22) sts. Work in St st, and *at the same time* inc 1 st fully fashioned (after the first st and before the last st of the row) at each side every 4 rows 0 (0, 2, 2) times, then every 6 rows 9 (9, 8, 8) times—36 (38, 40, 42) sts. Cont even in St st until piece measures 18" (45.5 cm) from beg; end just having completed a WS row.

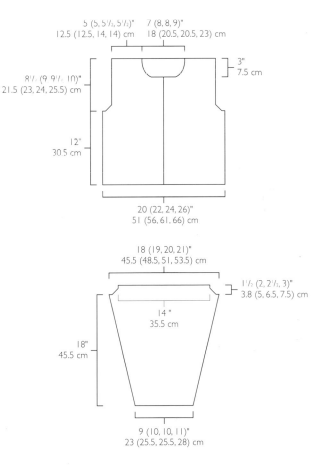

Shape sleeve cap: BO 2 sts at beg of next 2 rows—32 (34, 36, 38) sts. Cont in St st, dec 1 st at each side every RS row 2 (3, 4, 5) times as for back—28 sts rem when all decs have been completed. Work even in St st until sleeve cap measures 1½ (2, 2½, 3)" (3.8 [5, 6.5, 7.5] cm). BO all sts.

Finishing

Weave in ends. Block pieces to measurements. Sew shoulder seams.

Using the diagram below as a guide, with smaller crochet hook apply beaded metallic strand to body using tambour hook method, beading only every third chain st.

Set sleeves into armholes. Sew sleeve and side seams.

With RS facing and larger crochet hook, join chenille yarn to lower edge of jacket and work 1 row of sc evenly along the lower edge and around the entire front opening.

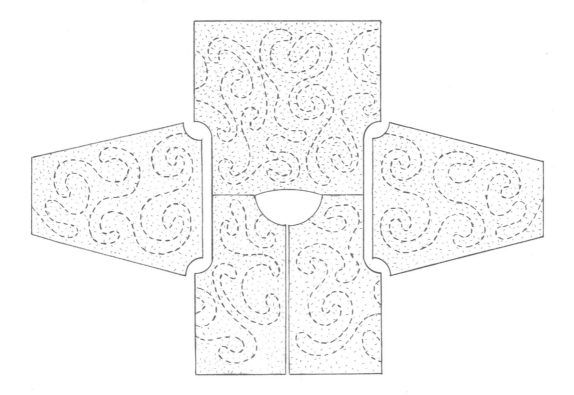

CHAPTER 10

Mixed Methods in Knitting

Cabled Tunic, Grace Kelly Collar

Why confine yourself to only one method within a project? Very often, mixing methods is advantageous. Rather than having to prestring beads in the exact reverse-order of appearance, use a different non-prestrung method to incorporate another bead color! Work some beads into the fabric, but experiment and embellish further, using an "after the fact" method. We have presented eight so far, so there are lots to choose from! Mix and match your methods for the desired effect and/or ease of use.

Cabled Tunic

Beads accentuate the stitches at the center of the cables in this elegant tunic. Beads also form their own zigzag pattern along the rib lines between the cables. Different sizes and colors of beads add more layers and hues to an already textured knit, and impart apparent complexity. This tunic is much easier to make than meets the eye, and such a classic will be enjoyed for years to come.

Finished Size

34 (39, 44, 49, 54)" (86.5 [99, 112, 124.5, 137] cm) bust/chest circumference. Tunic shown measures 39" (99 cm). This garment is intended to be standard fitting.

Materials

- Yarn: Classic Elite Miracle (50% alpaca, 50% Tencel; 108 yd [99 m]/50 g): #3329 Fundy Bay blue, 11 (12, 13, 14, 15) skeins.

- Beads: Size 3 or 5.5mm glass pebble beads: about 475 (560, 650, 675, 760). Shown in #05202 amethyst, from Mill Hill/Gay Bowles Sales. Size 6 seed beads: about 2,000 (2,300, 2,700, 3,000, 3,450). Shown in cobalt blue with silver lining, from Sandaga.

- Needles: Size 6 (4 mm): straight and 16" (40-cm) circular (cir). Adjust needle size if necessary to obtain the correct gauge.

- Notions: Bead-stringing needle; steel crochet hook size 9 (1.25 mm) or smaller, or small bead hook; cable needle (cn); stitch markers; tapestry needle.

Gauge

24 sts and 36 rows = 4" (10 cm) in patt from charts; 15-st patt repeat measures 2½" (6.5 cm) wide; 6-st cable section = 1" (2.5 cm) wide; and 9-st zigzag rib section = 1½" (3.8 cm) wide.

Special Notes

Prestring forty 5.5mm glass beads on each skein of yarn before working, adding more if necessary from the end of the skein.

Slipped sts are slipped as if to purl.

Special Abbreviations

B1: Bead 1 (worked on WS rows). Place a size 6 seed bead on hook. Work to the stitch that will hold the bead, hook the top of the stitch, transfer the bead to the stitch by pushing it off the hook with your finger, and pull the top of the stitch up through the bead hole. Return the stitch to the left needle and purl it on the WS.

BUB: Bring Up Bead, snuggle the bead up close to the needle. On RS, work as p1, BUB, p1; each bead will lie on the yarn strand between the two purl stitches.

M1: Make 1 increase. With the left needle tip, lift the strand between the needles from front to back, and knit the lifted strand through the back loop to increase 1 st.

Back

CO 103 (118, 133, 148, 163) sts. Work Rows 1–3 from Back and Front chart once for lower edge. Rows 1–3 are written out in words as follows:

Row 1: (WS) P2, [k1, p1] 4 times, k1, *p2, k2, p2, [k1, p1] 4 times, k1; rep from * 6 (7, 8, 9, 10) times, p2.

Row 2: K2, *k1, sl 1 with yarn in back (wyib), k9, p2, k2; rep from * 6 (7, 8, 9, 10) times, k1, sl 1 wyib, k9.

Row 3: P2, [k1, p1] 3 times, k1, B1, k1, *p2, k2, p2, [k1, p1] 3 times, k1, B1, k1; rep from * 6 (7, 8, 9, 10) times, p2.

When Row 3 has been completed, rep Rows 4–27 for patt; do not rep Rows 1–3. Rows 4–27 are written out in words as follows:

Row 4: (RS) K2, *k3, sl 1 wyib, k5, sl 3 to cn and hold in back, k3, k3 from cn; rep from * 6 (7, 8, 9, 10) times, k3, sl 1 wyib, k7.

Row 5: P2, [k1, p1] 2 times, k1, B1, k1, p1, k1, *p6, [k1, p1] 2 times, k1, B1, k1, p1, k1; rep from * 6 (7, 8, 9, 10) times, p2.

Row 6: K2, *k5, sl 1 wyib, k9; rep from * 6 (7, 8, 9, 10) times, k5, sl 1 wyib, k5.

Row 7: P2, k1, p1, k1, B1, [k1, p1] 2 times, k1, *p6, k1, p1, k1, B1, [k1, p1] 2 times, k1; rep from * 6 (7, 8, 9, 10) times, p2.

Row 8: K2, *k7, sl 1 wyib, k3, p1, BUB, p1, k2; rep from * 6 (7, 8, 9, 10) times, k7, sl 1 wyib, k3.

Row 9: P2, k1, B1, [k1, p1] 3 times, k1, *p6, k1, B1, [k1, p1] 3 times, k1; rep from * 6 (7, 8, 9, 10) times, p2.

Rows 10 and 11: Rep Rows 6 and 7.

Rows 12 and 13: Rep Rows 4 and 5.

Row 14: K2, *k1, sl 1 wyib, k13; rep from * 6 (7, 8, 9, 10) times, k1, sl 1 wyib, k9.

Row 15: P2, [k1, p1] 3 times, k1, B1, k1, *p6, [k1, p1] 3 times, k1, B1, k1; rep from * 6 (7, 8, 9, 10) times, p2.

Row 16: K2, *k3, sl 1 wyib, k7, p1, BUB, p1, k2; rep from * 6 (7, 8, 9, 10) times, k3, sl 1 wyib, k7.

Row 17: Rep Row 5.

Rows 18 and 19: Rep Rows 6 and 7.

Row 20: K2, *k7, sl 1 wyib, k1, sl 3 to cn and hold in back, k3, k3 from cn; rep from * 6 (7, 8, 9, 10) times, k7, sl 1 wyib, k3.

Row 21, 22, and 23: Rep Rows 9, 10, and 11.

Row 24: Rep Row 16.

Row 25: Rep Row 5.

Rows 26 and 27: Rep Rows 14 and 15.

Repeat Rows 4–27 until piece measures 11¾ (11½, 11½, 12¼, 12)" (30 [29, 29, 31, 30.5] cm) from beg; end having just completed a WS row.

Shape armholes: Cont in patt, BO 8 (8, 8, 15, 15) sts at the beg of the next 2 rows—87 (102, 117, 118, 133) sts. Keeping 2 sts at each side in St st as before, cont in patt until armholes measure 7¼ (8½, 9½, 9¾, 11)" (18.5 [21.5, 24, 25, 28] cm), and end having just completed a RS row.

Shape back neck and shoulders: Cont in patt, work 30 (37, 45, 45, 53) sts, join second ball of yarn and BO center 27 (28, 27, 28, 27) sts, work in patt to end—30 (37, 45, 45, 53) sts at each side. *Note:* The rest of the neck shaping and shoulder shaping are worked at the same time; read the next section through to the end before proceeding. Working each side separately in patt, BO at each neck edge 4 sts once, 3 sts once, then 2 sts once, then dec 1 st from each neck edge once. *At the same time,* beg immediately after the center back neck BO row, work shoulder shaping by BO at each armhole edge 4 (5, 6, 6, 7) sts once, then 3 (4, 6, 5, 7) sts once, then 3 (4, 6, 6, 7) sts twice, then 3 (5, 5, 6, 7) sts once, then 4 (5, 6, 6, 8) sts once.

Front

Work same as back until armholes measure 5¼ (6½, 7½, 7¾, 9)" (13.5 [16.5, 19, 19.5, 23] cm); end having just completed a RS row—87 (102, 117, 118, 133) sts.

Shape front neck and shoulders: Cont in patt as established, work 35 (42, 50, 50, 58) sts, join a separate ball of yarn, BO center 17 (18, 17, 18, 17) sts, work in patt to end—35 (42, 50, 50, 58) sts at each side. *Note:* The rest of the neck shaping and shoulder shaping are worked at the same time; read the next section through to the end before proceeding. Working each side separately in patt, BO at each neck edge 3 once, then 2 sts once—30 (37, 45, 45, 53) sts at each side. Work fully fashioned decreases as fol-

lows every RS row 10 times total: On first shoulder work to last 3 sts, k2tog, k1; on second shoulder k1, ssk, work to end—10 sts decreased from each side of neck when all neck decreases have been completed. *At the same time,* when armholes measure 7¼ (8½, 9½, 9¾, 11)" (18.5 [21.5, 24, 25, 28] cm), work shoulder shaping as for back.

Sleeves

CO 40 (55, 55, 55, 70) sts. Work Rows 1–3 from sleeve chart once for lower edge. Rows 1–3 are written out in words as follows:

Row 1: (WS) P4, k2, p2, *[k1, p1] 4 times, k1, p2, k2, p2; rep from * 2 (3, 3, 3, 4) times, p2.

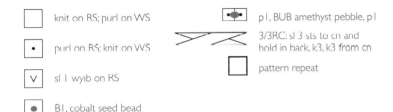

Back and Front

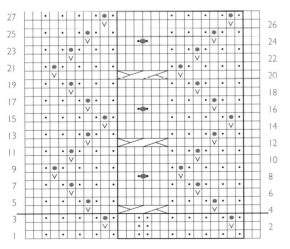

Sleeves

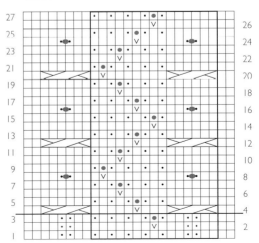

Row 2: K2, *k2, p2, k3, sl 1 with yarn in back (wyib), k7; rep from * 2 (3, 3, 3, 4) times, k2, p2, k4.

Row 3: P4, k2, p2, *[k1, p1] 3 times, k1, B1, k1, p2, k2, p2; rep from * 2 (3, 3, 3, 4) times, p2.

When Row 3 has been completed, rep Rows 4–27 for patt; do not rep Rows 1–3, and *at the same time* work a fully fashioned inc at each side on RS rows every 4 rows 1 (1, 17, 23, 28) time(s), then every 6 rows 12 (17, 13, 8, 3) times, then every 8 rows (11, (6, 0, 0, 0) times as foll: K2, M1, work to last 2 sts, M1, k2; work inc'd sts into patt as they become established—88 (103, 115, 117, 132) sts after all incs have been completed.

Rows 4–27 are written out in words as follows:

Row 4: (RS) K2, *sl 3 to cn and hold in back, k3, k3 from cn, k3, sl 1 wyib, k5; rep from * 2 (3, 3, 3, 4) times, sl 3 to cn and hold in back, k3, k3 from cn, k2.

Row 5: P8, *[k1, p1] 2 times, k1, B1, k1, p1, k1, p6; rep from * 2 (3, 3, 3, 4) times, p2.

Row 6: K2, *k11, sl 1 wyib, k3; rep from * 2 (3, 3, 3, 4) times, k8.

Row 7: P8, *k1, p1, k1, B1, [k1, p1] 2 times, k1, p6; rep from * 2 (3, 3, 3, 4) times, p2.

Row 8: K2, *k2, p1, BUB, p1, k9, sl 1 wyib, k1; rep from * 2 (3, 3, 3, 4) times, k2, p1, BUB, p1, k4.

Row 9: P8, *k1, B1, [k1, p1] 3 times, k1, p6; rep from * 2 (3, 3, 3, 4) times, p2.

Rows 10 and 11: Rep Rows 6 and 7.

Rows 12 and 13: Rep Rows 4 and 5.

Row 14: K2, *k7, sl 1 wyib, k7; rep from * 2 (3, 3, 3, 4) times, k8.

Row 15: P8, *[k1, p1] 3 times, k1, B1, k1, p6; rep from * 2 (3, 3, 3, 4) times, p2.

Row 16: K2, *k2, p1, BUB, p1, k5, sl 1 wyib, k5; rep from * 2 (3, 3, 3, 4) times, k2, p1, BUB, p1, k4.

Row 17: Rep Row 5.

Rows 18 and 19: Rep Rows 6 and 7.

Row 20: K2, *sl 3 to cn and hold in back, k3, k3 from cn, k7, sl 1 wyib, k1; rep from * 2 (3, 3, 3, 4) times, sl 3 to cn and hold in back, k3, k3 from cn, k2.

Row 21, 22, and 23: Rep Rows 9, 10, and 11.

Row 24: Rep Row 16.

Row 25: Rep Row 5.

Rows 26 and 27: Rep Rows 14 and 15.

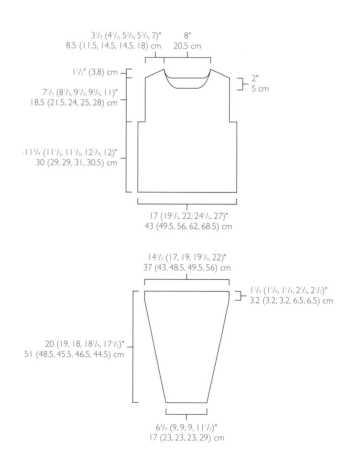

Cont in patt until piece measures 20 (19, 18, 18¼, 17½)" (51 [48.5, 45.5, 46.5, 44.5] cm) from beg. BO all sts. Mark each side of sleeve 1¼ (1¼, 1¼, 2½, 2½)" (3.2 [3.2, 3.2, 6.5, 6.5] cm) down from BO row for armhole placement.

Finishing

Weave in ends. Block pieces to measurements. Sew shoulder seams. Set BO edge of sleeves into armholes, and sew straight portion at top of sleeves (above markers) to BO armhole sts. Sew sleeve and side seams.

Neckband

Using cir needle and RS facing, beg at right shoulder seam, pick up and knit 53 (52, 53, 52, 53) sts across back neck, then pick up and knit 67 (68, 67, 68, 67) sts evenly across around front neck—120 sts. Sl sts from left to right needle tip until you are at the beg of a 9-st zigzag rib section. Rejoin yarn and place marker to indicate beg of round (rnd). Working in the rnd with the RS of piece facing you at all times, beg with Row 4, work the red patt rep box of the back and front chart 8 times around, aligning the cable and zigzag rib sections with the body. Rows 4–22 are written out in words for working in the rnd as follows:

Rnd 4: *K3, sl 1 wyib, k5, sl 3 to cn and hold in back, k3, k3 from cn; rep from * around.

Rnd 5: *P1, k1, p1, B1, [p1, k1] 2 times, p1, k6; rep from * around.

Rnd 6: *K5, sl 1 wyib, k9; rep from * around.

Rnd 7: *[P1, k1] 2 times, p1, B1, p1, k1, p1, k6; rep from * around.

Rnd 8: *K7, sl 1 wyib, k3, p1, BUB, p1, k2; rep from * around.

Rnd 9: *[P1, k1] 3 times, p1, B1, p1, k6; rep from * around.

Rnds 10 and 11: Rep Rnds 6 and 7.

Rnds 12 and 13: Rep Rnds 4 and 5.

Rnd 14: *K1, sl 1 wyib, k13; rep from * around.

Rnd 15: *P1, B1, [p1, k1] 3 times, p1, k6; rep from * around.

Rnd 16: *K3, sl 1 wyib, k7, p1, BUB, p1, k2; rep from * around.

Rnds 17, 18, and 19: Rep Rnds 5, 6, and 7.

Rnd 20: *K7, sl 1 wyib, k1, sl 3 to cn and hold in back, k3, k3 from cn; rep from * around.

Rnd 21: Rep Rnd 9.

Rnd 22: Rep Rnd 6.

Neckband measures about 2" (5 cm). BO all sts in patt. Weave in ends.

Grace Kelly Collar

This very dramatic piece will dress up any simple dress or top. Wear it over a basic black sheath for evening. Pair it with a pastel top for afternoon tea. Such a small piece gets a lot of bang for the buck and it knits up very quickly, too. The use of a twisted stitch before and after the stranded beads keeps them locked in place. Three types of beads embellish the novel tape/ribbon yarn.

Finished Size
About 4" (10 cm) deep, 15" (38 cm) around at inner neck, and 39" (99 cm) around at outer neck.

Materials
- Yarn: Jaeger Albany (100% mercerized cotton tape; 115 yd [105 m]/50 g): #226 misty, 1 skein. Yarn distributed in U.S. by Westminster Fibers.
- Beads: Size 6 glass seed beads: about 1,750. Shown in #16602 white ice, from Mill Hill/Gay Bowles Sales. Size 3 or 5.5mm glass pebble beads: about 140. Shown in #05161 clear frost, from Mill Hill/Gay Bowles Sales. Size 5mm pearl teardrop pendants: about 70. Beads shown from Sandaga, style number not available.
- Needles: Size 5 (3.75 mm): straight. Adjust needle size if necessary to obtain the correct gauge.
- Notions: Bead-stringing needle; crochet hook size G (4.5 mm); steel crochet hook size 6 (1.75 mm) or smaller, or small bead hook; coordinating fabric-covered hook-and-eye closure (the kind used for fur coats); tapestry needle; sharp-pointed sewing needle and matching thread (to attach clasp).

Gauge
22 sts = 4" (10 cm) in St st.

Special Notes
Always knit the first and last stitches of each row for selvedge stitches.

The reverse stockinette stitch side of the work is intended to be worn as the public side of the collar.

Special Abbreviations
BUB: Bring Up Bead, snuggle the bead up close to the needle. Each bead will lie on the yarn strand between two stitches. When BUB is followed by a number, it means to bring up that number of prestrung seed beads between the stitches.

B1: Bead 1, worked on a WS row. Place bead on hook; either large clear seed bead (L), or pearl teardrop (T) will be specified. Work to the stitch that will hold the bead, hook the top of the stitch, transfer the bead to the stitch by pushing it off the hook with your finger, and pull the top of the stitch up through the bead hole. Return the stitch to the left needle and k or p st according to patt. For teardrop beads, make sure the bead hangs to the correct side of the work.

Instructions

Prestring size 6 glass seed beads onto yarn before working. CO 216 sts using the chain cast-on as follows:

Chain cast-on

Make slipknot and place on the larger crochet hook. With hook in right hand and knitting ndl in left, *bring yarn behind ndl from below and to front from above ndl. Catch yarn with hook and pull through to form a ch—1 st CO. Rep from * until there are 215 sts chained on the ndl. Place remaining ch from hook onto ndl as last st—216 sts.

Row 1 (RS): K1, *p1 tbl, B1 T, p1, B1 T, p1 tbl, BUB 9, drop 6 chained cast-on sts from ndl leaving a long swag between the sts on either side; rep from * to last st, ending k1 instead of BUB 9—102 sts.

Row 2 (WS): K1, *k1 tbl, k3, k1 tbl, BUB 9; rep from *, to last st, ending k1 instead of BUB 9.

Row 3: K1, *p1 tbl, p3, p1 tbl, BUB 8; rep from *, end k1 instead of BUB 8.

Row 4: K1, *k1 tbl, k1, B1 L, k1, k1 tbl, BUB 8; rep from *, end k1 instead of BUB 8.

Row 5: K1, *p1 tbl, p3, p1 tbl, BUB 7; rep from *, end k1 instead of BUB 7.

Row 6: K1, *k1 tbl, k3, k1 tbl, BUB 7; rep from *, end k1 instead of BUB 7.

Row 7: K1, *p1 tbl, p3, p1 tbl, BUB 6; rep from *, end k1 instead of BUB 6.

Row 8: K1, *k1 tbl, k1, B1 L, k1, k1 tbl, BUB 6; rep from *, end k1 instead of BUB 6.

Rows 9 and 10: Rep Rows 5 and 6, but BUB 5 instead of BUB 7.

Rows 11 and 12: Rep Rows 7 and 8, but BUB 4 instead of BUB 6.

Rows 13 and 14: Rep Rows 5 and 6, but BUB 3 instead of BUB 7.

Rows 15 and 16: Rep Rows 7 and 8, but BUB 2 instead of BUB 6.

Rows 17 and 18: Rep Rows 5 and 6, but BUB 1 instead of BUB 7.

Row 19: K1, *p1 tbl, p3, p1 tbl; rep from *, end k1.

Row 20: Knit across.

Row 21: (Decrease Row) K1, p4, *p2tog, p3; rep from *, end p1, k1—83 sts.

Row 22: *K3, B1 T; rep from *, end k3.

Row 23: Knit across.

Row 24: (Eyelet Row) K1, *p2tog, yo; rep from *, end p1, k1.

Row 25: Knit across.

Row 26: *K1, B 1 L; rep from *, end k1.

Bind off as if to knit on next row.

Finishing

Weave in ends. Sew hook-and-eye closure securely to ends of collar on the wrong side, just below the bind-off row.

CHAPTER II

Crocheting with Beads in Chain Stitch

Amulet Bag

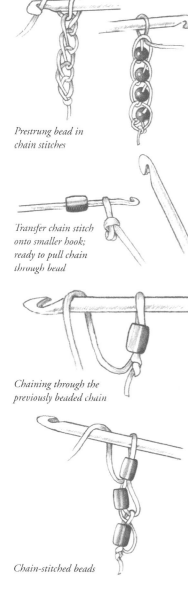

Prestrung bead in chain stitches

Transfer chain stitch onto smaller hook; ready to pull chain through bead

Chaining through the previously beaded chain

Chain-stitched beads

Many of the techniques for Beaded Knitting can be adapted to crochet; the between-stitches method of Chapter 2, the hooked-on method of Chapter 6, the separate strand method of Chapter 7, the sewing method of Chapter 8, and the tambour method of Chapter 9.

Because there are more ways to form basic stitches in crochet (chain, slip stitch, single crochet, half-double crochet, double crochet, treble crochet, etc.), as opposed to just knitting or purling, the crochet chapters are broken down into stitch type. Variations, such as prestrung and applied methods, are found within each chapter.

Let's begin with the basic foundation for all crochet, the humble chain stitch.

Prestrung (see Chapter 1), the bead falls on the bumpy part in the back of a chain. Form a slipknot and place on hook. Bring the bead up close to the hook, then wrap the yarn around the hook and draw through the slipknot to form the chain. * Bring a bead up close to the hook, then wrap the yarn around the hook and draw through the loop already on the hook. Repeat from *.

Applied, the bead covers up almost all of the chain. Form a slipknot and place on hook. Wrap the yarn around the hook and draw through the slipknot to form the chain. * Place the bead on the mini-latch hook or crochet hook (see Chapter 6), and push the bead downward onto the chain stitch until the whole chain stitch is pulled through the hole of bead.

Transfer loop back to regular hook. Wrap the yarn around the hook and draw through the loop already on the hook to form a chain. Repeat from *.

Of course, not every chain needs to have a bead on it. For a sparser look, the beading may be done in either method every few chains or so.

The sparse method involves a lot of stopping and starting, as well as a lot of transfer of tools. The prestrung method entails a lot of shoveling down of beads. It also means that the back side is usually the right side, since this is where the beads wind up. The hooked-on method is more reversible, with the bead just about covering up the whole stitch in the round.

Amulet Bag

Is this an oversized necklace or very little purse, you ask? It's a bit of both! Borrowed from the many knitted versions, this can be a vessel for small treasures for crocheters, too. Try using random, multicolored beads. Fun, quick, and easy to make, this bag is an ideal gift. Who can resist?

Finished Size
4" (10 cm) wide × 2¾" (7 cm) deep excluding strap.

Materials
- Yarn: Skacel's Manuela No.10 (100% cotton, 305 yd [279 m]/50 g), # M032 Nachtblau, 1 skein.

- Beads: Size 11 glass seed beads: about 958 fuchsia silver-lined, style number and source not available.

- Crochet hook: Steel crochet hook size 7 (1.5 to 1.75 mm). Adjust size if necessary to obtain correct gauge.

Notions
Bead-stringing needle; tapestry needle.

Gauge
9 sts and 9 rows sc = 1" (2.5 cm)

Special Notes
Prestring half the beads on yarn before working. After working halfway, cut yarn and prestring same number for other half.

WS of work always faces you.

Special abbreviations
BUB—Bring Up Bead, snuggle the bead up close to the hook. Beads lie on yarn strand behind ch.

Bch: Beaded chain. BUB, wrap the yarn over hook and through loop already on hook.

Top Chain
Make slipknot, place on hook, *BUB, ch 1 (bch formed), rep from * until there are 36 bch's, join with slip st to first bch being careful not to twist ch.

Strap
Work 100 beaded chs for strap, skip 18 beaded chs of top ch, join with sl st to next beaded ch to attach other end of strap.

Body
Rnd 1: Ch 1, sc in same ch as slip st, *work bch, skip next ch, sc in each of next 2 ch; rep from *, ending with sc in last ch, do not turn, do *not* join work. From here on, work in rounds, marking beg/end of rounds with contrasting piece of yarn.

Rnds 2, 3, 4, and 5: *Sc in next sc, work bch, skip next ch, sc in next sc; rep from * around.

Rnd 6: *Sc in next sc, work 2 bch, skip next ch, sc in next sc; rep from * around.

Rnds 7, 8, 9, and 10: *Sc in next sc, work 2 bch, skip next 2 ch, sc in next sc; rep from * around.

Rnd 11: *Sc in next sc, work 3 bch, skip next 2 ch, sc in next sc; rep from * around.

Rnds 12, 13, 14, and 15: *Sc in next sc, work 3 bch, skip next 3 ch, sc in next sc; rep from * around.

Rnd 16: *Sc in next sc, work 4 bch, skip next 3 ch, sc in next sc; rep from * around.

Rnds 17, 18, 19, and 20: *Sc in next sc, work 4 bch, skip next 4 ch, sc in next sc; rep from * around.

Rnd 21: *Sc in next sc, work 5 bch, skip next 4 ch, sc in next sc; rep from * around.

Rnds 22, 23, 24, and 25: *Sc in next sc, work 5 bch, skip next 5 ch, sc in next sc; rep from * around.

Joining row: With WS of bag facing out, flatten bag—beg/end of rounds become the right-hand fold. Insert hook into first sc from WS on front and into last sc from RS on back of bag, sc these 2 sts tog, *work 5 beaded ch, skip next 5 bch on front and back; working through double thickness, insert hook into next sc from WS on front and into next corresponding sc from RS on back, sc these 2 sts tog; insert hook into next sc from WS and into next corresponding sc from RS, sc these 2 sts tog, rep from * across bottom edge of bag; end with sc in last sc, fasten and end off. Turn bag right-side-out.

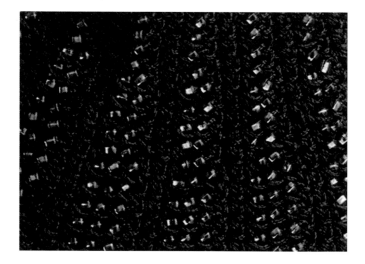

CHAPTER 12

Crocheting with Beads in Single Crochet
PDA Cover/Purse, Suspended in Space Stole

Prestrung bead in single crochet

Prestrung bead between single crochets

In single crochet, there are many ways of getting beads onto the fabric. Let's start with the prestrung methods.

In single crochet, the bead is most commonly applied to the back of the stitch. Insert the hook to a stitch and draw up a loop (there are now two loops on the hook). Bring the bead up close to the hook, yarn around the hook, and draw through both loops on hook to complete the single crochet with a bead on the back.

As with knitting, one can also place a bead between each of the single crochet stitches. Upon completing a single crochet, bring a bead up close to the hook before commencing with the next single crochet.

The bead sits more squarely on a stitch in the first "back of stitch" method. It is also more secure. In the second "between stitches" method, the bead is a little off-kilter between stitches. The beads slant to the right in the back-of-stitch method, to the left in the between-stitches method.

An interesting effect occurs when both methods are combined! A zigzag, almost herringbone-like quality emerges. It makes for a very dense fabric.

In both these fabrics, the beads sit on the back. When you're working back-and-forth (as opposed to in the round), the beads in back mean that they show up only every other row. Bead every row and the fabric becomes reversible, yet the beads are offset, lying to one side on rows 1, 3, 5, etc., and to the other side on rows 2, 4, 6, etc. This alternation also results in a very dense fabric.

If you want to bead on every row and you don't want to work in the round, you should employ a flipped stitch. Normally, the hook is inserted in a stitch from front to back. In a flipped stitch, the hook is inserted in a stitch from back to front. The yarn then begins on the front rather than on the back.

Draw a loop through the stitch; the loop now ends up on the back of the fabric toward the wrong side. Bring a bead up close to the hook, then yarn around the hook, and draw through both loops on the hook to complete the flipped single crochet.

Now the bead lies to the front (or right side) of the fabric. If you're using the between-stitches method, the bead must lie between *two* flipped single crochet stitches. Work a flipped single crochet, bring a bead up close to the hook, then work another flipped single crochet on the right side rows.

Inserting hook for flipped, beaded single crochet

Another way of getting a bead to the front of the fabric is the applied method. Again, using the hooked-on method (similar to the techniques discussed in Chapters 6 and 11), insert the hook in a stitch and pick up a loop. Place this loop on a very fine hook with a bead on it. Push the bead down onto the picked-up loop. Return to your regular hook. Yarn around the hook and draw through both loops to complete the single crochet.

If you want a bead in the back when working a wrong side row using this applied method without prestringing, employ the flipped single crochet stitch again. With the yarn in the front, insert the hook in a stitch *from back to front* and

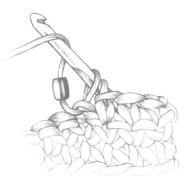

Loop drawn through, ready to complete stitch with bead

Hooked onto flipped single crochet from wrong side

Hooked onto single crochet from right side

Alternate behind stitch and between stitch from wrong side

Bead between single crochet, worked from wrong side

Bead behind single crochet, worked from wrong side

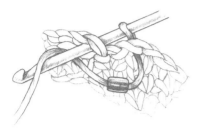

Bead lies between two flipped single crochets

Hooking-on bead in single crochet

pick up a loop. Place this loop on a very fine hook with a bead on it. Push the bead down onto the picked-up loop.

Return to your regular hook. Yarn around the hook and draw through both loops to complete the single crochet.

The pictured swatches show a regular hooked bead worked from the right side, then a hooked bead on a flipped single crochet worked from the wrong side. Both methods get the bead to the right side.

These different methods result in different vertical placement on the stitch. The applied method of hooking a bead onto the picked-up loop, either regular or flipped, makes the bead sit on the stitch in the lowest possible position. The between-stitches method places the bead a little higher up on the stitch. The bead in the sitting-atop-a-stitch method lies closest to the top of the stitch.

Picked-up loop with bead back onto hook, ready to complete stitch

Placing bead onto picked-up loop in flipped single crochet

Picked-up loop with bead back onto hook, ready to complete stitch

PDA Cover/Purse

By day, this is a dressy PDA (personal digital assistant) holder. By night, it's the perfect evening purse. Make the straps shorter for wearing around the neck, longer for slinging over the shoulder. Make two separate shorter straps and tie it around your waist! Wear several together in different colors. Decisions, decisions. . . .

Finished Size

4¼" (11 cm) wide × 5" (12.5 cm) tall, excluding cord.

Materials

- Yarn: Skacel's Manuela No.10 (100% cotton, 305 yd [279 m]/50 g), # M012 garnet, 1 skein.

- Beads: Size 11 glass seed beads: about 2,700. Shown in #00081, from Mill Hill/Gay Bowles Sales. Teardrop beads, silver metal, #ME814-S: 12 beads, from Shipwreck Beads.

- Crochet hook: Steel crochet hook size 6 (1.75 mm). Adjust hook size if necessary to obtain correct gauge.

Gauge

9 sc and 9 sc rows = 1" (2.5 cm) in patt.

Special Notes

Prestring beads on yarn before working. Prestring 927 seed beads for flap and bag back. After working these sections, cut yarn and prestring 724 seed beads for bag front, then string [5 seeds, 1 teardrop, 5 seeds] 12 times for fringed bottom trim.

Special Abbreviations

BUB: Bring Up Bead, snuggle the bead up close to the hook. Beads lie on yarn strand behind sc.

BU3B: Bring up 3 seed beads.

BU5seed, teardrop, 5seedB: Bring up (5 seed, 1 teardrop, 5 seed) beads.

Bsc: Beaded single crochet, pick up loop in next st, BUB, yarn around hook and draw through both loops on hook to complete st.

Bfsc: Beaded flipped single crochet, have yarn in front, insert hook in next st from back to front, pick up loop, BUB, yarn around hook and draw through both loops on hook to complete st.

Buttonloop

Ch 1, [BUB, ch 1] to form beaded ch, work another 11 beaded ch's—1 ch and 12 beaded ch. Join with slip st to first ch to form circle, being careful not to twist.

Flap

Row 1: (RS) Ch 1, work 3 sc in ch of joined slip st.
Row 2: BU3B, ch 1 and turn, 2 sc in first sc to inc, Bsc in next sc, 2 sc in last sc to inc—5 sts.
Row 3: BU3B, ch 1 and turn, inc in first st, Bfsc in each of next 3 sc, inc in last st—7 sts.
Row 4: BU3B, ch 1 and turn, inc in first st, Bsc in each of next 5 sc, inc in last st—9 sts.

Row 5: BU3B, ch 1 and turn, sc in each of first 3 sc, Bfsc in each of next 3 sc, sc in each of last 3 sc—9 sts.

Row 6: BU3B, ch 1 and turn, sc in each of first 4 sc, Bsc in next sc, sc in each of last 4 sc—9 sts.

Row 7: BU3B, ch 1 and turn, inc in first st, Bfsc in next sc, sc in each of next 5 sc, Bfsc in next sc, inc in last st—11 sts.

Row 8: BU3B, ch 1 and turn, inc in first st, Bsc in each of next 3 sc, sc in each of next 3 sc, Bsc in each of next 3 sc, inc in last st—13 sts.

Row 9: BU3B, ch 1 and turn, inc in first st, Bfsc in next in each of next 5 sc, sc in next sc, Bfsc in each of next 5 sc, inc in last st—15 sts.

Row 10: BU3B, ch 1 and turn, [sc in each of next 3 sc, Bsc in each of next 3 sc] twice, sc in each of last 3 sc—15 sts.

Row 11: BU3B, ch 1 and turn, sc in each of first 4 sc, Bfsc in next sc, sc in each of next 5 sc, Bfsc in next sc, sc in each of last 4 sc—15 sts.

Rows 12–29: Work foll chart—39 sc on Row 29.

Rows 30–41: Work foll chart on 39 sts.

Rows 42–71: Rep Rows 32 to 41 3 times.

Rows 72 and 73: Work foll chart. Cut yarn and prestring 724 seed beads for bag front, then string [5 seeds, 1 teardrop, 5 seeds] 12 times for fringed bottom trim.

Row 74: (Fringe Row, WS) Ch 1 and turn, *sc in next 3 sc, BU5seed, teardrop, 5seedB; rep from * across, end with sc in each of last 3 sc.

Rows 75 and 76: Work foll chart.

Rows 77–116: Rep Rows 32 to 41 4 times.

Rows 117–119: Work foll chart.

Row 120: Sl st in each st across.

Finishing

Block piece. Line if desired. Sew up sides. Weave in ends.

Cord

Prestring about 900 beads on yarn. Leaving a 12" [30.5 cm] sewing length, ch 6, join with slip st to first ch to form circle, being careful not to twist. From here on, work in rounds without joining with a slip st or turning work, using contrasting yarn to mark beg/end of rounds.

Row 1: (WS) Ch 1, *sc in next ch, Bsc in next ch; rep from * around, do not join—3 sc and 3 bsc.

Row 2: *Sc in next ch, Bsc in next ch; rep from * around.

Rep Row 2 until cord measures 24" (61 cm) or desired length (if longer, more beads are required), fasten and end off leaving a 12" (30.5 cm) sewing length. Using sewing lengths, sew each end of cord to top sides of bag.

Button

Prestring 40 seed beads on yarn.

Do not join rounds but mark them with piece of contrasting yarn. Make slipknot with about 4"–6" (10–15 cm) tail, keep tail in *front* of work at all times. *Note:* Wrong side is on outside of tube at all times.

Rnd 1: (WS) Ch 2, 8 Bsc in second ch from hook, do not join.

Rnd 2: 2 Bsc in each sc around—16 sc.

Rnd 3: Bsc in each sc around—16 bsc.

Rnd 4: *Sc in next sc, skip next sc; rep from * around—8 sc.

Rnd 5: *Skip next sc, sl st in next sc; rep from * around—4 sl sts, fasten and, end off yarn leaving 6" (15 cm) tail, tie both beg and end tails tightly tog in square knot, tie ends to center front of bag to correspond with buttonloop.

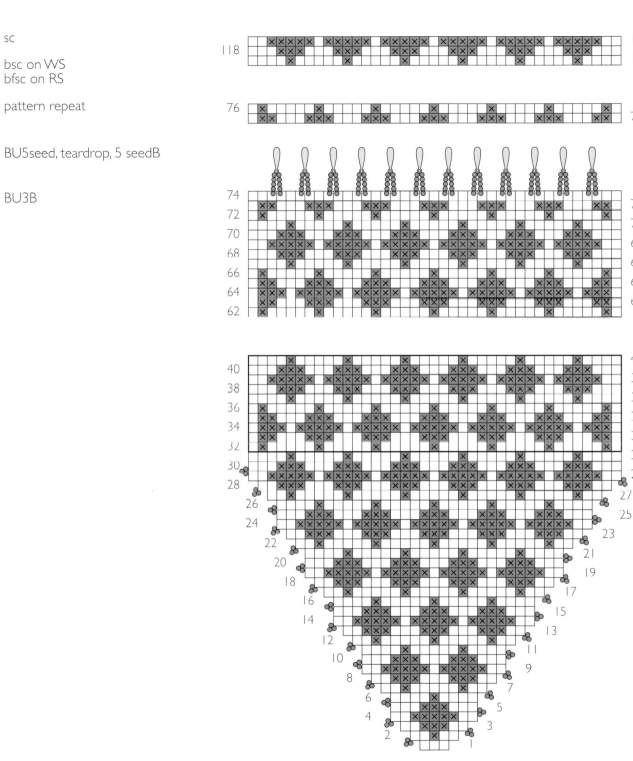

sc

bsc on WS
bfsc on RS

pattern repeat

BU5seed, teardrop, 5 seedB

BU3B

Suspended in Space Stole

Soft yet strong, light yet hefty, lacy yet warm, a stunning stole is *de riguer* for tossing around shoulders, waist, or even just the back of a chair. Crochet a narrow version for a scarf. For pure luxury, create a very wide version for the sofa!

Finished Size

17¼" (44 cm) wide and 60" (152.5 cm) long, excluding fringe.

Materials

- Yarn: Karabella Lace Mohair (61% superkid mohair, 8% wool, 31% polyamid; 540 yd [494 m]/50 g): #3087 lipstick red, 1 skein.

- Beads: Size 6 glass seed beads: about 1,300. Shown in gold, from Sandaga.

- Crochet hook: Size F/8 (4 mm). Adjust hook size if necessary to obtain the correct gauge.

- Notions: American Beadle (mini-latch hook, see Chapter 8) or small steel crochet hook size 10 (1 mm) or fine tapestry needle.

Gauge

Four 6-st rep ([ch 5, sc in center of ch-5 lp of previous row] 4 times, for 24 sts total) = 3" (7.5 cm) and 5 rows = 2" (5 cm) in mesh stitch pattern. Exact gauge is not critical for this project.

Special Notes

Begin stole at center back. Complete the first half and fasten off. To start the second half, work into the foundation chain of the first half.

Beads are attached to sc on the RS of the work. Start sc in usual manner by inserting hook through work, wrapping yarn over hook and pulling to front of work, wrap yarn over hook and pull through loop. Place bead on mini-latch hook or small steel crochet hook. Transfer picked-up lp to small steel hook, push bead onto picked-up lp, place lp back on regular hook and complete sc.

Special Abbreviations

Bch: Beaded chain. Ch 1, place bead on mini-latch hook or small steel crochet hook. Transfer lp to small steel hook, push bead onto lp, place lp on regular hook to continue.

Mesh Pattern

Row 1: (WS) Sc in 2nd ch from hook, *ch 5, sk 3 ch, sc in next ch; rep from *.

Row 2: Ch 5 and turn (counts as a dc and ch-2), *sc in center ch of next ch-5 lp, ch 5; rep from *, end ch 2, dc in last sc.

Row 3: Ch 1 and turn, sc in first dc, *Ch 5, sc in center ch of next ch-5 lp; rep from * across.
Rep Rows 2 and 3 for patt.

First Half

Ch 94 loosely (foundation ch made).

Row 1: (WS) Work as for Row 1 of mesh patt—23 ch-5 lps.

Row 2: Work as for Row 2 of mesh patt, placing beads on first and every alternate sc.

Row 3: Work as for Row 3 of mesh patt—23 ch-5 lps.

Row 4: Work as for Row 2 of mesh patt, placing beads on
second and every alternate sc.

Row 5: Rep Row 3.

Rep Rows 2 to 5, working even in mesh patt as established, foll stole chart until piece measures 30" (76 cm),
ending with Row 2 or Row 4 (beading row). Fasten off.

Last Row: Repeat Row 3, working ch-3 lps instead of
ch-5 lps.

Second Half

With WS facing, join yarn to first ch of foundation ch at
start of first half.

Row 1: (WS) Ch 1, sc in same ch as join, *ch 5, sk 3 ch,
sc in next ch; rep from *, turn—23 ch-5 lps.

Work in mesh patt (starting with Row 2) and beg foll
stole chart for bead placement as for first half.

Work second half same as first half to end. Turn, do
not fasten off.

Fringe

Rnd 1: (RS) Ch 1, sc in first sc, *work 7 bch, sk ch-3 lp,
sc in next sc; rep from * to end—23 beaded lps, with
RS still facing, pivot stole and sc evenly across long
side edge, pivot stole and work fringe across other
short end, pivot stole and with RS still facing, sc
evenly across other long side edge, and fasten off.
Weave in loose ends.

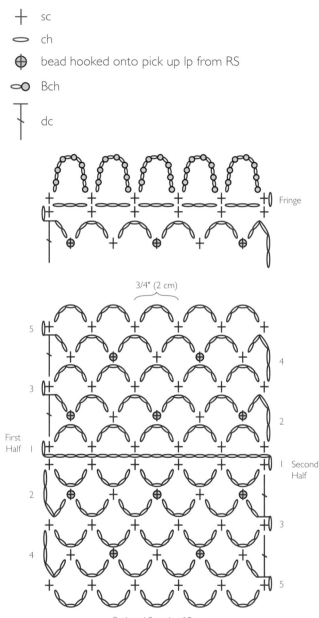

+	sc
⬯	ch
⊕	bead hooked onto pick up lp from RS
⊸○	Bch
⊤	dc

Reduced Sample of Patt

Half-double crochet bead variations:

Bead hooked onto flipped half-double crochet from wrong side

Bead hooked onto half-double crochet on right side

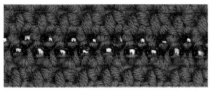

Alternate behind and between half-double crochet on wrong side

Bead between half-double crochet on wrong side

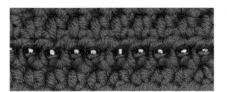

Bead behind back of half-double crochet on wrong side

Wrapping yarn the opposite direction in flipped half-double crochet

CHAPTER 13

Crocheting with Beads in Half-Double Crochet

I'm Biased Headband and Wristlets

This is an easy one! Take what you learned in the previous chapter on single crochet and just substitute half-double crochet. After all, half-double crochet is nothing but a single crochet with an extra yarn around the hook. This is done at the beginning before inserting the hook in a stitch to draw up a loop.

Thus, the prestrung methods are all the same: The bead sits to the back atop a stitch, the bead sits to the back between stitches, the bead sits in the front atop a stitch if the flipped half-double crochet is employed, and the bead sits in the front between stitches if the flipped half-double crochet is employed on either side of the bead.

The applied methods with a hook are also the same: The bead sits in the front atop a stitch and the bead sits to the back atop a stitch if the flipped half-double crochet is employed.

The one difference between beads in single crochet and beads in half-double crochet is in the flipped stitches. In half-double crochet, wrap the yarn around the hook in the opposite direction than normal, before inserting the hook in a stitch from back to front, since the yarn begins in the front of the fabric.

One other slight difference between beads in single crochet and beads in half-double crochet is that in half-double crochet, beads on the prestrung between-stitches method lie higher up on the stitch than the prestrung on-the-stitch method. Beads added in the applied or hooked method lie the lowest on the stitch, with the flipped stitch being higher up than the regular one.

I'm Biased Headband and Wristlets

I'm not biased, but these versatile accessories are! Size them up or down with ease for every member of the family. To put a slant in your athletic gear, make these in cotton. Miniversions of this pattern make great napkin rings! Super-size the band to get a cowled neck-warmer. Even use it as trim for the bottoms of sweaters and cuffs. Gather the top of a large band to make a dirndl skirt. Add a crown and you've got a hat. A long, narrow version can become a sock top. Are you starting to get the idea?

Finished Sizes
Wristlets: 3" (7.5 cm) deep and 7" (18 cm) circumference. Headband: 2½" (6 cm) deep and 21½" (54.5 cm) circumference.

Materials
- Yarn: Lion Brand Woolease Sport (80% acrylic, 20% wool; 435 yd [398 m]/140 g): #107 blue bell, 1 skein.
- Beads: Size 6 glass seed beads about 900. Shown in #F24 cool mosaic, from Toho Shoji.
- Crochet hook: Size F/5 [3.75 mm]. Adjust hook size if necessary to obtain the correct gauge.
- Notions: Bead-stringing needle; tapestry needle.

Gauge
20 sts and 15 rows = 4" (10 cm) in pattern (working through back loops).

Special Notes
Prestring beads on yarn before working. Prestring 209 beads for each cuff. Prestring 231 for half the headband. After working halfway, cut yarn and prestring same number for other half.

Special Abbreviations
BUB: Bring Up Bead. Snuggle the bead up close to the hook. Beads will lie on the RS on the yarn strand behind the hdc.

Bhdc: Beaded half double crochet. Yarn around hook, pick up lp in next st, BUB, yarn around hook and draw through all three lps on hook to complete st.

Cuffs
Ch 20 loosely, BUB, ch 1.

Row 1: (WS) Yarn around hook, pick up lp in second ch from hook, yarn around hook, pick up lp in next ch, yarn around hook and draw through all 5 lps on hook (a dec), work bhdc in each of next 17 ch, bhdc in last ch, work regular hdc in last ch to inc—20 hdc, 18 are beaded, end hdc's are not.

Row 2: BUB, ch 1, work 2 hdc in first hdc, hdc tbl of next 17 hdc, yarn around hook, pick up lp in back lp of next hdc, yarn around hook, pick up lp through both lps of last hdc, yarn around hook and draw through all 5 lps on hook (a dec)—20 hdc.

Row 3: BUB, ch 1, yarn around hook, pick up lp in first hdc, yarn around hook, pick up lp tbl of next hdc,

yarn around hook and draw through all 5 lps on hook (a dec), work bhdc in back lp of each of next 17 hdc, bhdc through both lps of last hdc, work regular hdc in last hdc to inc—20 hdc, 18 are beaded, end hdc's are not.

Rep Rows 2 and 3 for patt.

When there are 22 rows total worked, fasten off leaving 12" (30.5 cm) tail. With tail, working in back lps of sts, sew last row to beg foundation ch to form tube.

Headband

Ch 15 loosely, BUB, ch 1.

Row 1: (WS) Yarn around hook, pick up lp in second ch from hook, yarn around hook, pick up lp in next ch, yarn around hook and draw through all 5 lps on hook (a dec), work bhdc in each of next 13 ch, bhdc in last ch, work regular hdc in last ch to inc—15 hdc, 13 are beaded, end hdc's are not.

Row 2: BUB, ch 1, work 2 hdc in first hdc, hdc tbl of next 13 hdc, yarn around hook, pick up lp tbl of next hdc, yarn around hook, pick up lp through both lps of last hdc, yarn around hook and draw through all 5 lps on hook (a dec)—15 hdc.

Row 3: BUB, ch 1, yarn around hook, pick up lp in first hdc, yarn around hook, pick up lp tbl of next hdc, yarn around hook and draw through all 5 lps on hook (a dec), work bhdc in back lp of each of next 13 hdc, bhdc through both lps of last hdc, work regular hdc in last hdc to inc—15 hdc, 13 are beaded, end hdc's are not.

Rep Rows 2 and 3 for patt.

When there are 66 rows total worked, end off leaving 12" (30.5 cm) tail. With tail, working in back lps of sts, sew last row to beg foundation ch to form tube.

CHAPTER 14

Crocheting with Beads in Double Crochet

Plum Lines Vest

Bead behind upper part of double crochet

Bead behind lower part of double crochet

Flipped double crochet

The longer the crochet stitch, the more the variations grow, almost exponentially. As with previous chapters, let's start with the prestrung options. With double crochet, there are two stitch heights—upper and lower. Wrap yarn around the hook (Step 1), and pick up a loop (Step 2) in a stitch. Yarn around the hook and draw through two loops (Step 3), and then yarn around the hook again to draw through the remaining two loops (Step 4).

There are opportunities every step of the way to insert the beads. Traditionally, the bead is placed at the upper position. That is, after Step 3, bring the bead up close to the hook before proceeding with Step 4.

Yet there is no reason why the bead cannot be brought up after Step 2 and before Step 3. The bead is then positioned behind the double crochet in the lower position.

Already, the possibilities are coming fast and furious. Try a row of alternating uppers and lowers. Try a row of two consecutive uppers alternating with two consecutive lowers, or three uppers and three lowers. Make them syncopated—for instance, three uppers and a lower, then one upper and a lower, etc.

Place a bead in both the upper and lower position on the same double crochet stitch! This technique makes for a dense fabric, so do it only every other stitch or every third or fourth stitch, etc.

To work this technique on the right side and have the bead facing you (in front of the stitch rather than in back), again employ the flipped method as described in the previous chapters. As with half-double crochet, work Step 1 in the opposite direction, then work Step 2 by inserting the hook in the stitch from back to front to pick up a loop.

At this point, there's a choice. Place the bead before drawing through the first two loops (for lower position) or place the bead before drawing through the last

Beads hooked to upper position in front of trc

Beads hooked to mid-position in front of trc

Beads hooked to lower position in front of trc

Beads in all three positions behind trc

Beads in middle and upper positions behind trc

Beads in lower and middle position behind trc

Beads in highest and lowest position in trc

Bead behind trc lower position

Bead behind trc middle position

Bead behind trc upper position

Bead between trc lower position

Bead between trc upper position

Flipped dc from WS, hooked to upper part of dc

Flipped dc from WS, hooked to upper part of dc

Applied bead hooked over upper part of dc

Applied bead hook over lower part of dc

Dc in back of both upper and lower part of st

Same as left, but add between upper part of st

Dc in back of upper part of st

Dc in between lower part of st

Dc in back of lower part of st

Dc in back of upper part of st

Dc between upper part of st

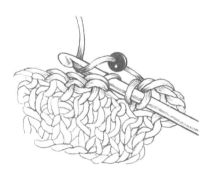

Bead between lower part of double crochet

two loops (for upper position). This is how beads are able to show up on every row—both right and wrong side rows—when you're working back and forth.

Then there are the between-stitches methods. After completing one double crochet, bring the bead up close to the hook before proceeding with the next double crochet. This step results in a bead that very clearly looks as if it is stationed between each stitch, rather than squarely sitting on the stitch. Its position is slightly higher than that of the upper-position beaded double crochet.

Yet it is possible to bring the bead up in another, lower position. I call this the between-the-stitch-lower, since it is not on either legs of Steps 3 and 4. Push the bead up within Step 2. That is, after Step 1, insert the hook in the stitch, place the bead up close to the hook before bringing the yarn around the hook to pull up a loop to complete Step 2.

Doing this places the bead on the other leg at the bottom of the stitch, similar to the behind-double crochet stitch in the lower position.

Some may say this is splitting hairs (or yarn, as the case may be!). Nevertheless, I want to arm you with as many options as possible. For instance, combine this last method with the first and second methods in this chapter to form a miniature triangle of beads on the same double crochet stitch!

Of course, to work any of these from the right side and to have the bead sit in front of a stitch, do the flipped version of double crochet.

The applied method of using the hook generally follows the same principles. Hook the bead to the bottom of the front of the stitch after Step 2 and before Step 3. Hook the bead to the top of the front of the stitch after Step 3 and before Step 4. Hook the bead to the bottom of the back of the stitch using the flipped method, again between Steps 2 and 3. Hook the bead to the top of the front of the stitch using the flipped method between Steps 3 and 4.

At this point, let me make a token mention of treble crochet (trc). Though I do not devote a chapter to this technique, I wrote at the very beginning of this chapter that the longer the stitch, the greater the possibilities. With three "heights," the variations grow even more! I've pictured several options, but see how many variations you can come up with on your own!

Plum Lines Vest

Slimming lines and striking graphics make this vest a year-round favorite. Wear it as a sleeveless top or as a vest over another garment. Make it long and it's a sheath dress or jumper.

Finished Size

34½ (40, 45, 50½)" (87.5 [101.5, 114.5, 128.5] cm) bust/chest circumference. This garment is intended to be loose fitting. Vest shown measures 40" (101.5 cm).

Materials

- Yarn: Lion Brand Woolease Sport (80% acrylic, 20% wool; 435 yd [398 m]/140 g): #147 boysenberry, 2 (2, 3, 4) skeins.

- Beads: Size 6 glass seed beads: about 850 (1,050, 1,250, 1,500). Shown in color #18FAB lime, from Beads World.

- Crochet hook: Size H/8 (5 mm). Adjust hook size if necessary to obtain the correct gauge.

- Notions: Bead-stringing needle; yarn needle.

Gauge

3 shell sts and 10 rows in shell patt = 4" (10 cm).

Special Notes

Prestring beads on yarn before working. Prestring half the front/back with 213 (263, 313, 350) beads. After working half the vest, cut yarn and prestring another 213 (263, 313, 350) beads for other half.

Front is slightly longer than back to accommodate back-neck drop.

Special Abbreviations

BUB: Bring Up Bead, snuggle the bead up close to the hook. Beads will lie on the RS on the yarn strand behind the dc.

Special Stitches

Shell: 5 double crochet in same st.

Bdc: Beaded double crochet, yarn around hook, pick up loop in next st, [BUB, yarn around hook and draw through 2 loops on hook] twice to complete st.

Beaded Shell: [Dc, bdc, dc, bdc, dc] all in same st.

Back

Trim

Very loosely ch 80 (92, 104, 116).

Row 1: (WS) Sc in second ch from hook, *skip 2 ch, work beaded shell in next ch, skip 2 ch, sc in next ch **, skip 2 ch, work shell in next ch, skip 2 ch, sc in next ch; rep from * across, ending last rep at **—13 (15, 17, 19) shell sts total.

Row 2: Ch 3 (counts as dc) and turn, work another 2 dc in first sc (half-shell made), *skip 2 dc, sc in next dc (the center dc of 5-dc shell), skip 2 dc, work 5 dc in next sc; rep from * across, end with only 3 dc in last sc (half-shell made)—12 (14, 16, 18) shell sts total with a half-shell at each end.

Row 3: Ch 1 and turn, sc in first dc, *skip 2 dc, work shell in next sc, skip 2 dc, sc in next dc (the center dc of 5-dc shell), skip 2 dc, beaded shell in next sc, skip 2 dc, sc in next dc (the center dc of 5-dc shell); rep from * across, end by skipping next 2 dc, work shell in next sc, skip next 2 dc, sc in top of turning ch-3.

Row 4: Rep Row 2.

Row 5: Ch 1 and turn, sc in first dc, *skip 2 dc, work beaded shell in next sc, skip 2 dc, sc in next dc (the center dc of 5-dc shell), skip 2 dc, work shell in next sc, skip 2 dc, sc in next dc; rep from * across, end last sc in top of turning ch-3.

Rep Rows 2 to 5 for patt. Work until 17 rows total have been completed, ending with a Row 5 of patt.

Body

Rep Rows 4 and 5 alternately. Work until 37 rows total have been completed, ending with a Row 5 of patt.

Shape for Armhole: (RS) Turn, slip st into first sc and next 3 dc (dec half-shell made), ch 1, sc in same dc as last sl st (the center dc of 5-dc shell), cont row in established patt, end with sc in center dc of last shell, do not work rem 2 dc and sc (dec half-shell made)—12 (14, 16, 18) shell sts total.

Rep last row 3 more times—9 (11, 13, 15) shell sts total at end of last row.

Cont to work even in established patt, with RS rows having 8 (10, 12, 14) shells with a half-shell at each end, and WS rows having 9 (11, 13, 15) shell sts, until a total of 55 (57, 59, 61) rows have been completed.

Front

Work as for back until there are 48 (50, 52, 54) rows total, ending with a RS row.

Shape Neck: Keep to established patt and work first 4 (5, 6, 7) shells, skip next [2 dc, sc and 2 dc], join another strand of yarn with 32 (40, 48, 60) beads prestrung on it to next dc, ch 1, sc in same dc and complete row in established patt—4 (5, 6, 7) shells on each shoulder.

Working both shoulders at same time, keep to established patt, dec 1 half-shell at neck edge on each of next 5 rows (1½ [2½, 3½, 4½] shells at end of last row). Work even

in patt on 1½ (2½, 3½, 4½) shells until 58 (60, 62, 64) rows have been completed, ending with a WS row. Fasten and end off, leaving a long sewing length on each shoulder.

Finishing

Block pieces to measurements. Sew shoulder seams. Sew side seams.

Neck Trim

With RS facing, join yarn in shoulder seam on neck edge, ch 1, sc evenly around neck opening, sl st in first sc to join, fasten and end off.

Armhole Trim

With RS facing, join yarn in side seam of armhole, ch 1, sc evenly spaced around armhole edge, sl st in first sc to join, fasten and end off. Rep armhole trim around other armhole.

Bottom Trim

With RS facing, join yarn in first ch on opposite side of foundation ch, ch 1, sc in first ch, skip next 2 ch, shell in next ch, skip next 2 ch, *sc in next ch, skip next 2 ch, shell in next ch, skip next 2 ch, rep from * around bottom edge, sl st in first sc to join. Weave in ends.

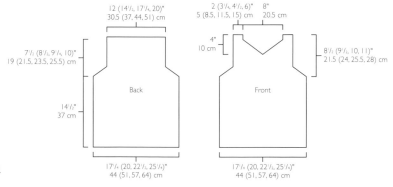

12 (14½, 17¼, 20)"
30.5 (37, 44, 51) cm

2 (3¼, 4½, 6)" 8"
5 (8.5, 11.5, 15) cm 20.5 cm

4"
10 cm

7½ (8½, 9¼, 10)"
19 (21.5, 23.5, 25.5) cm

8½ (9½, 10, 11)"
21.5 (24, 25.5, 28) cm

Back

Front

14½"
37 cm

17¼ (20, 22½, 25¼)"
44 (51, 57, 64) cm

17¼ (20, 22½, 25¼)"
44 (51, 57, 64) cm

CHAPTER 15

True Bead Knitting in Crochet

Floral Beaded Pockets

You can make a total beaded fabric of crochet much like true Bead Knitting. A bead lies on each and every stitch on each and every row. As with bead knitting, the yarn is not visible from the right side.

Use the chart from Chapter 5 (see page 46). Bead up the exact same sequence. Regular beaded single crochet from the wrong side and flipped beaded single crochet from the right side keep the beads on the same surface when you're working back and forth flat (refer to Chapter 12). Interestingly enough, this pattern gives a left and right slant to the alternate rows of beads, not unlike that of plaited bead knitting.

If a piece is worked circularly in the round, the wrong side always faces, regular beaded single crochet is used, and charts are always read from right to left. This technique forms a bias or torque, much like the back-loop-only method in knitting. Images are distorted. To see similar effects, refer to the spiral cord of the PDA Cover/Purse of Chapter 12 (see page 96) or Cleopatra's Asp from Chapter 18 (see page 139).

Because even short single crochet is slightly taller than a knit stitch, this beaded pocket is more elongated than any of the knitted ones. If the length poses a problem, redo the chart with fewer rows.

Floral Beaded Pockets

It is my personal opinion that an allover beaded fabric is far easier to crochet than it is to knit. You can achieve results similar to true bead knitting with far less time and effort. The silk yarn employed here infuses suppleness into the crochet, which normally does not drape as much as knitting. Like the knitted pockets, make a matching sweater to put the pocket on, or make two pockets and sew them up to create a purse.

Finished Size

3¾" (9.5 mm) wide and 4" (10 mm) high.

Materials

- Yarn: Gudebrod Silk size F (100% silk; 140 yd [128 m]/spool): #12–1164BS Z ivory, 1 spool. Yarn distributed by Fire Mountain Gems.

- Beads: Glass seed beads (see Floral Beaded Pockets knitted instructions of Chapter 5, page 42)

- Crochet hook: Steel size 6 (1.75 mm). Adjust hook size if necessary to obtain the correct gauge.

- Notions: Bead-stringing needle; tapestry needle.

Gauge

43 sts and 49 rows = 4" (10 cm)

Special Note

Prestring beads on yarn before working in exact re-verse-order; see knitted pocket instructions (Chapter 5, page 42).

Special Abbreviations

BUB: Bring Up Bead. Snuggle the bead up close to the hook. Beads will lie to the RS of the fabric.

Bsc: Beaded single crochet. Pick up lp in next st, BUB, yarn around hook and draw through both lps on hook to complete st.

Bfsc: Beaded flipped single crochet. With yarn in front, insert hook in next st from back to front, pick up lp, BUB, yarn around hook and draw through both lps on hook to complete st.

Instructions

Set-up Row: (RS) Ch 41, sc in 2nd ch from hook and in each ch across—40 sc.

Ch 1 and turn. Keeping first and last st with no beads, begin chart from Chapter 5 (see page 46) on WS, Row 1, working regular Bsc on WS rows and Bfsc on RS rows until chart is completed and beads run out. Work 1 row of plain sc, fasten and end off.

CHAPTER 16

Mixed Methods in Crochet

Crocheted Choker and Necklace

In crochet, the use of different stitches almost defines the way a bead is placed on the project—but not quite. Of course, by the technique's very nature, using different stitches within a project alters the look and placement of the beads. A bead placed higher up on a double crochet may lie next to a bead lower down on a single crochet. This necklace employs beads in both chain stitches, as well as regular and flipped double crochet.

Remember that there are prestrung methods, as well as applied or hooked-on methods. The possibilities have expanded greatly as you've been introduced to the varied techniques in this book. So, which method do you choose and why? As with knitting, rather than having to prestring beads in exact reverse order of appearance, use another non-prestrung method to attach another color of bead!

Not covered here, but certainly an option, is to work some beads integrally into the fabric, embellishing further with sewing or tambour embroidery (discussed in Chapters 8 and 9).

Crocheted Choker and Necklace

Two versions are shown here, one for a thick strand in cotton and one for a thin strand in pure silk. Both are closed with a real jewelry clasp for a luxurious feeling and ease in putting on and removing.

Finished Size

12" (30.5 cm) long and ½" or 1" (1.3 or 2.5 cm) high.

Materials

- Yarn: Choker—Gudebrod Silk Thread size E (100% silk; 200 yd [183 m]/spool); #12–1127BS brown, 1 spool. Necklace—Skacel Manuela size 10 (100% cotton; 305 yd [279 m]/50 g): # M021 strato, 1 skein.

- Beads: Choker—Size 12 glass seed beads: about 400. Shown in #601 copper, from Beads World. Necklace—Size 11 glass seed beads: about 325. Shown in #02021 charcoal, from Mill Hill/Gay Bowles Sales.

- Crochet hook: Choker—Steel size 9 (1.4 mm). Necklace—Steel size 6 (1.75 mm). Adjust hook sizes if necessary to obtain the correct gauge.

- Notions: Gold or silver metal clasp; sharp-pointed sewing needle and matching thread (to attach clasp).

Gauge

Version 1 (Brown silk thread)—10 rows = 3" (7.5 cm). Version 2 (Strato cotton thread)—8 rows = 3" (7.5 cm).

Special Note

Prestring beads on yarn before working.

Special Abbreviations

BUB: Bring Up Bead. Snuggle the bead up close to the hook. Beads will lie on the RS on the yarn strand behind the dc.

Fdcdb: Flipped double crochet with double beads. Yarn around hook in opposite direction and insert hook into st from back to front rather than front to back, [BUB, yarn around hook and draw through 2 loops] twice to complete dc.

Dbdc: Double-bead double crochet. Yarn around hook and insert hook in st and pick up lp, [BUB, yarn around hook and draw through 2 loops] twice to complete dc.

Instructions

Row 1: (RS) Ch 4 (counts as a dc), [fdcdb, dc, ch 2, dc, fdcdb, dc] all in fourth ch from hook.

Row 2: Ch 3 and turn, *[BUB, ch 1] 3 times, sl st into third ch of beg ch 3*, [BUB, ch 1] 5 times, sl st into third ch of beg ch 3, rep from * to *, ch 2, skip 3 dc, [dc, dcdb, dc, ch 2, dc, dcdb, dc] all in next ch-2 space.

Row 3: Turn, sl st into each of first 3 dc, sl st into ch-2
    space, ch 3 (counts as a dc), [fdcdb, dc, ch 2, dc,
    fdcdb, dc] all in ch-2 space.
Rep Rows 2 and 3 for patt.
    Work until piece measures 12" (30.5 cm) or desired
length, ending with Row 2. Fasten and end off.

Finishing
Block piece if desired. Sew clasps to ends.

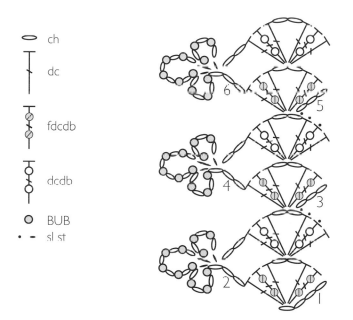

- ch
- dc
- fdcdb
- dcdb
- BUB
- sl st

CHAPTER 17

Extras for Knitting and Crocheting: Looping Techniques, Bugles, Spangles

Burnished Metal Lariat/Belt, Shimmy Camisole

Leaving Long Loops for Latching Up Later

In either knitting or crochet, leaving a long loop of many prestrung beads normally makes fringe. But you can also hike up this beaded loop and work it into the fabric, instead of letting it dangle.

An even number of beads creates a dead-center space for hiking up the loop. In knitting, one may leave the long loop between the stitches (either in knit or purl), as described in Chapter 2. Because of the substantial volume of the loop, the beads will even stay to the right side of stockinette! You may also leave the long loop in front of a slipped stitch as described in Chapter 3.

Work the loop row by placing several beads in a long loop and repeating this as desired across a row. Work a few rows plain or in pattern. Work up to the stitch where you will secure the loop. Hike up the long loop by treating it as a very long stitch and working it together with another stitch as follows:

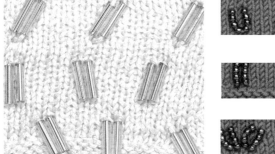

Knit loops on right side as "fringe" in front of single slipped stitch

Knit loops on right side in front of single slip stitch, hiked-up vertically

Knit loops on right side between knit stitches, hiked-up diagonally

Knitted bugle beads as long loops

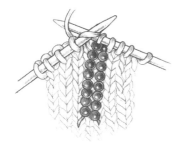

Hiking up in knit with loop in front

Hiking up in knit with loop in back

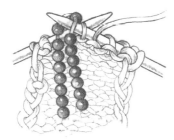

Hiking up in purl with loop in front

Hiking up in purl with loop in back

Knit with the loop in front of the work. Insert right-hand needle into the long loop from front to back in a knit-wise fashion, go into the next stitch (also with right-hand needle), knit both long loop and stitch together.

Knit with loop in back of the work. Lift long loop with right-hand needle from *behind* up and onto left-hand needle, and knit both long loop and next stitch together.

Purl with loop in front. Insert right-hand needle into stitch as if to purl, then into long loop from back to front, and purl both long loop and next stitch together.

Purl with loop in back. Lift long loop with right-hand needle from *behind* up and onto left-hand needle, purl both long loop and next stitch together.

In crochet, one may leave the long loop between the stitches on either side. Again, because of the substantial volume of the loop, the beads will stay in front of the fabric in any stitch.

One may also skip some stitches to accommodate the long loop (just remember to regain them later to avoid losing stitches, unless you want a decrease).

Work the loop row by forming the long loop with several beads. Work a few rows plain or in pattern. Work up to the stitch where the hike is desired. Hike up the long loop by treating the loop as a very long stitch and working it together with another stitch as follows.

Forming crochet loops in front of single crochet

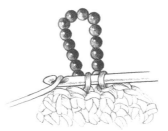

Forming crochet loops in back of single crochet

Sc with loop in front. Insert hook into the long loop from front to back, insert hook into next stitch, draw yarn through both stitch and long loop, yarn around hook and draw through both loops on hook to complete stitch.

Sc with loop in back. Insert hook into next stitch, insert hook into the long loop from front to back, draw yarn through both stitch and long loop, yarn around hook and draw through both loops on hook to complete stitch.

Notice how the between-stitches loops have no direct stitch above to hike up to. Instead, you must either leave the loops as free-floating fringe or hike up on a diagonal (to the left or right). When you're hiking up on a diagonal, the further away the stitch is from the loop origin, the longer the loops should be. Obviously, the more beads left in the loop, the longer the loop. Furthermore, the longer the loop, the more rows there are between the loop-forming row and the hike-up row.

Somewhat unique to crochet is the ability to form longer stitches, such as double crochet (though one can argue that knit stitches with multiple wraps create a similar effect). In the pictured swatch, hiked-up long loops take the place of a double crochet with empty spaces of chains to either side and produce a lacy effect.

Bugle Beads

A bugle bead is a long bead (see Raj Pillow from Chapter 8). By its very length, this bead distorts most knit or crochet stitches. It may be used, however, in front of several knitted slip stitches, not unlike the Afro-centric Vest with Wooden Beads from Chapter 3. The bugle bead is ideal for long loops, however, because of its length. Thus, treat a bugle bead as though it is several beads clustered together!

Unfortunately, the hole of the bugle bead is not very big. This means you have to use awfully thin yarn. As you can see in the picture, the bugles may be left dangling like fringe. They may also be hiked up in the same manner as a long loop. Using an even number of bugle beads leaves a space in the dead-center of the stitch.

My Burnished Metal Lariat/Belt uses two bugle beads instead of a loop of several smaller beads as a double crochet substitute.

Hiking up in single crochet with loop in front

Hiking up in single crochet with loop in back

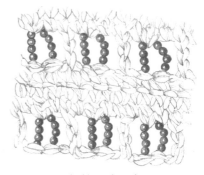

Long loop as double crochet substitute

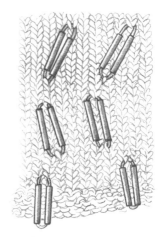

Long loops as double crochet substitute

Knit with spangle in front

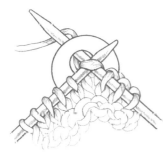

Knit with spangle in back

Purl with spangle in front

Purl with spangle in back

Spangles/Paillettes

Spangles, also known as paillettes, are big sequins with an enlarged hole off-center and close to the edge. While technically not beads, spangles do add texture and a touch of glitz, and they're a lot of fun to knit or crochet.

Because they are usually sewn onto fabric, spangles often have pinholes instead of enlarged holes, but you can enlarge a pinhole by using an old-fashioned hole puncher. Since the spangle material is basically plastic or Mylar, it is easy to alter in this manner. The hole should be large enough to accommodate yarn and a knitting needle or crochet hook.

In knitting, there are four basic maneuvers:

Knit with spangle in front. Hold the spangle in front of the next stitch, insert right-hand needle in the hole of the spangle as if to knit, then insert right-hand needle in next stitch, and knit both stitch and spangle off together.

Knit with spangle in back. Hold the spangle in back of the next stitch, insert right-hand needle in next stitch, then insert right-hand needle in the hole of the spangle as if to knit, and knit both stitch and spangle off together.

Purl with spangle in front. Hold the spangle in front of the next stitch, insert right-hand needle in next stitch, then insert right-hand needle in the hole of the spangle as if to purl, and purl both stitch and spangle off together.

Purl with spangle in back. Hold the spangle in back of the next stitch, insert right-hand needle in the hole of the spangle as if to purl, then insert right-hand needle in next stitch, and purl both stitch and spangle off together.

The method to use is predicated on which is the right side, what row you're doing, and what stitch you are working. Notice, though, how the purl version is anchored down more securely at the top of the spangle hole. There are actually two strands holding it down. In knitting, the spangle has more movement and is able to shimmy and shine (think car wash).

In crochet, one can work the spangle in the back or front of a stitch, regardless of what stitch is being worked. Do this during insert-the-hook-in-stitch process.

To work a spangle in front of a stitch. Hold spangle in front of stitch, insert hook in hole of the spangle from front to back, then insert hook in stitch itself, draw yarn through both stitch and spangle, and complete stitch.

Crochet with spangle in front

To work a spangle in back of a stitch. Hold spangle in back of stitch, insert hook in stitch itself, then insert hook in hole of the spangle from front to back, draw yarn through both spangle and stitch, and complete stitch.

Crochet with spangle in back

As with knitting, the spangle behind the stitch moves less and the spangle in front of the stitch moves more.

If the hook or needle is too large to go through the spangle hole, use a smaller hook or needle to draw the stitch through the spangle, then place the drawn-through stitch on the larger working hook or needle.

Burnished Metal Lariat/Belt

The fabric of this slinky necklace or belt must be felt to be believed! Composed of almost all bugle beads and worked in silk, it can be expanded into a camisole or tank top. The long bugle beads emulate the long stitches of double crochet.

Finished Size

3¾" (9.5 cm) wide and 45" (114.5 cm) long.

Materials

- Yarn: Gudebrod Silk size F (100% silk; 140 yd [128 m]/spool): #12–1153BS 0 Brown, 1 spool. Yarn distributed by Fire Mountain Gems.

- Beads: 0.4" (1 cm) glass bugle beads: about 1,450. Shown in #611 copper, from Beads World.

- Crochet hook: Steel size 4 (2 mm). Adjust hook size if necessary to obtain the correct gauge.

- Notions: Bead-stringing needle; tapestry needle.

Gauge

16 sts = 1" (2.5 cm) and 18 rows = 4" (10 cm) in patt.

Special Note

Prestring bugle beads onto yarn before working with about 650 at beg of first spool, then 340 for the end of first spool and 418 at beg of second spool.

Special Abbreviations

BU2BB: Bring Up 2 Bugle Beads. Snuggle the 2 beads up close to the hook.

Instructions

Row 1: Chain 50, sc in 2nd ch from hook and in each ch across—49 sc.

Row 2: Ch 1 and turn, sc in each of first 4 sc, *BU2BB, skip next sc, sc in each of next 3 sc; rep from *, end sc in last sc—11 pairs of bugle beads forming V-lps.

Row 3: Ch 3 and turn (counts as a dc), skip first sc, dc in next sc, ch 2, skip next 2 sc, *sc into thread at center of next V-lp, ch 3, skip next 3 sc; rep from *, end sc into thread at center of last V-lp, ch 2, skip next 2 sc, dc in each of last 2 sc.

Row 4: Ch 1 and turn, sc in each of first 2 dc, 2 sc in next ch-2 space, *sc in next sc above V-lp, 3 sc in next ch-3 space; rep from *, end sc in next sc above last V-lp, 2 sc in next ch-2 space, sc in next dc, sc in top of turning ch—49 sc.

Rep Rows 2 to 4 for patt.

Work until one spool has run out; join other spool and cont patt. Work until bugle beads run out, ending with patt Row 4, rotate scarf and work 1 row of sc evenly spaced along one side edge working extra sc into corners. Rotate scarf and sc in each foundation ch, rotate scarf and sc evenly spaced along other side edge. Join with sl st to first sc of last completed row; fasten and end off.

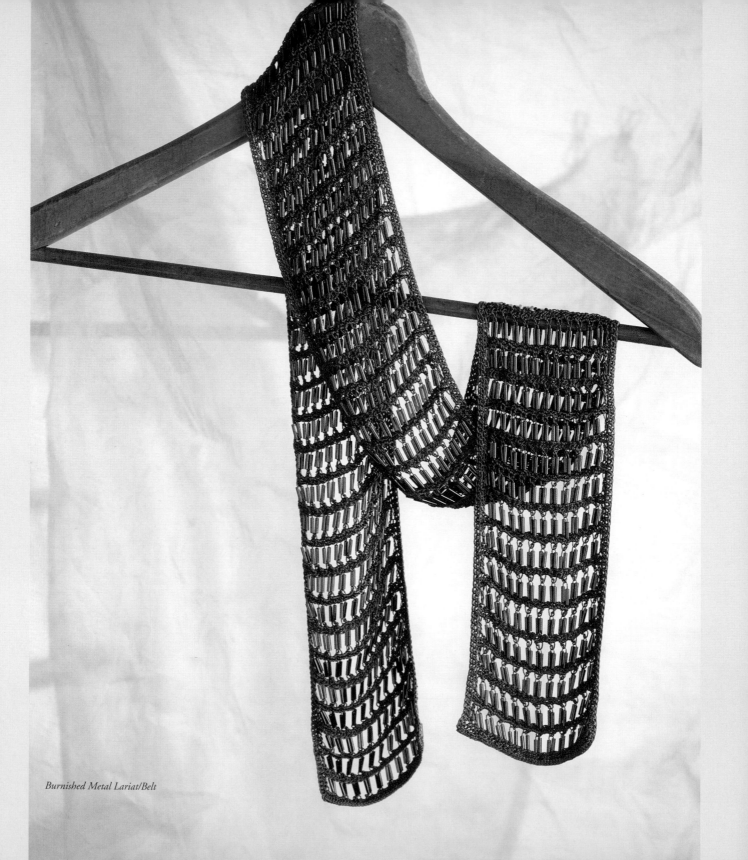

Burnished Metal Lariat/Belt

Shimmy Camisole

Spangles need not always be shiny. These matte ones still shimmy with movement and have plenty of glam, echoed by the slinky, variegated ribbon yarn. While the lustrous spangles yield dazzling brilliance at night, the matte spangles on this off-the-shoulder camisole move effortlessly from day to evening.

Finished Sizes

34 (36, 38, 40, 42)" (86.5 [91.5, 96.5, 101.5, 106.5] cm) bust/chest. This is intended to be a close-fitting garment.

Materials

- Yarn: Anny Blatt Victoria (100% nylon ribbon; 109 yd [100 m]/50 g), #283 jardin, 9 (10, 11, 12, 13) skeins.

- Spangles: ¾" (2 cm) in diameter, matte gray-beige, about 450 (460, 475, 485, 500), from Beads World.

- Crochet hooks: Sizes H/8 (5 mm), I/9 (5.5 mm) and J/10 (6 mm). Adjust hook sizes if necessary to obtain correct gauge.

Gauge

18 sc and 20 sc rows = 4" (10 cm) with small hook; 16 sc = 4" (10 cm) with medium hook; 14 sc = 4" (10 cm) with large hook.

Special Note

Body is worked in the rnd, but rnds are joined and turned. Work is then divided and front and back are worked separately in rows.

Special Abbreviation

Ssc: Spangled single crochet. With spangle in front, sc into spangle hole and next sc together.

Body

With small hook, loosely ch 154 (162, 170, 180, 190); very carefully join without twisting with sl st to first ch to form a circle.

Rnd 1: (RS) Ch 1, sc in ea ch around, join with sl st to first sc—154 (162, 170, 180, 190) sc.

Rnd 2: Ch 1 and turn, sc in ea ch around placing contrasting piece of yarn or st marker between center 2 sts to mark for side "seam," join with sl st to first sc. Continue to carry marker up each rnd.

Rnd 3: Ch 1 and turn, sc in ea ch around, join with sl st to first sc.

Rep Rnds 2 and 3 once.

Shape waist: Working in established patt, *at the same time* dec after first st and before last st, and dec second and third st before and after side-seam marker on fifth row, then every fourth row once, then every third row 5 times—126 (134, 142, 152, 162) sts. Work even until piece measures 7" (18 cm) total.

Shape bust: Inc after first st and before last st and inc in second st before and after side-seam marker on next row, then every fourth row 6 more times—154 (162, 170, 180, 190) sc. Work even until piece measures 14" (35.5 cm) total, ending with a WS row.

Shape back armholes: With RS facing sl st into each of next 4 (5, 6, 7, 8) sts, ch 1, sc in each of next 69 (71, 73, 76, 79) sts, leave rem sts unworked. Ch 1 and turn, work a WS row.

Next RS Row: (Dec Row) Ch 1 and turn, sc in first st, dec next 2 sc tog, sc across to within last 3 sc, dec next 2 sc tog, sc in last sc—67 (69, 71, 74, 77) sts.

Work in established patt, dec 1 sc at each end of every other row 5 (5, 3, 1, 1) more time(s), then every 3rd row 3 (3, 5, 7, 7) more times—51 (53, 55, 58, 61) sts, end ready to work a RS row.

Shape back neck: Ch 4 and turn (counts as a trc), skip first sc, trc in each of next 6 (6, 6, 7, 7) sc, dc in each of next 7 (7, 7, 8, 8) sc, hdc in each of next 7 (7, 7, 8, 8) sc, sc in each of next 9 (11, 13, 10, 13), hdc in each of next 7 (7, 7, 8, 8) sc, dc in each of next 7 (7, 7, 8, 8) sc, then trc in each of rem 7 (7, 7, 8, 8) sc, fasten and end off.

Shape front armholes: With RS facing, skip 8 (10, 12, 14, 16) sc from last st of first row of back armhole, join yarn in next sc, ch 1 and sc in same st and in each of next 68 (70, 72, 75, 78) sts—69 (71, 73, 76, 79) sts, leave rem 4 (5, 6, 7, 8) sts unworked.

Sizes 34", 36", and 38" Only: Work 1 row even in sc, then dec 1 sc at each end of next 2 rows. Rep last 3 rows 3 times—53 (55, 57) sts at end of last row.

Sizes 40" and 42" Only: Dec 1 sc at each end of every row 8 times—(60, 63) sts at end of last row.

All Sizes: Work 1 row even in sc, dec 1 sc at each end of next row—51 (53, 55, 58, 61) sts, ending with a WS row.

Shape front neck: Work as for back neck.

Finishing

Block piece to measurements.

Collar: With largest hook, loosely ch 144 (148, 152, 156, 160), very carefully join without twisting with sl st to first ch to form a circle.

Rnd 1: (RS) Ch 1, sc in ea ch around—144 (148, 152, 156, 160) sc, join with sl st to first sc.

Rnd 2 and all even numbered rnds: Ch 1 and turn, sc in ea ch around, join with sl st to first sc.

Rnd 3: (Spangle Row A) Ch 1 and turn, sc in first sc, *Ssc in next sc, sc in each of next 3 sc; rep from * around, end with Ssc in next sc, sc in each of last 2 sc, join with sl st to first sc.

Rnd 5: (Spangle Row B) Ch 1 and turn, sc in each of first 3 sc, *Ssc in next sc, sc in each of next 3 sc; rep from * around, end with Ssc in last sc, join with sl st to first sc.

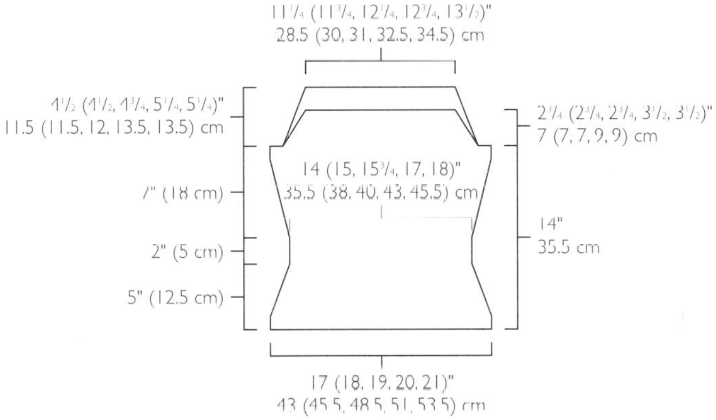
11 1/4 (11 3/4, 12 1/4, 12 3/4, 13 1/2)"
28.5 (30, 31, 32.5, 34.5) cm
4 1/2 (4 1/2, 4 3/4, 5 1/4, 5 1/4)"
11.5 (11.5, 12, 13.5, 13.5) cm
2 3/4 (2 3/4, 2 3/4, 3 1/2, 3 1/2)"
7 (7, 7, 9, 9) cm
14 (15, 15 3/4, 17, 18)"
35.5 (38, 40, 43, 45.5) cm
7" (18 cm)
14"
35.5 cm
2" (5 cm)
5" (12.5 cm)
17 (18, 19, 20, 21)"
43 (45.5, 48.5, 51, 53.5) cm

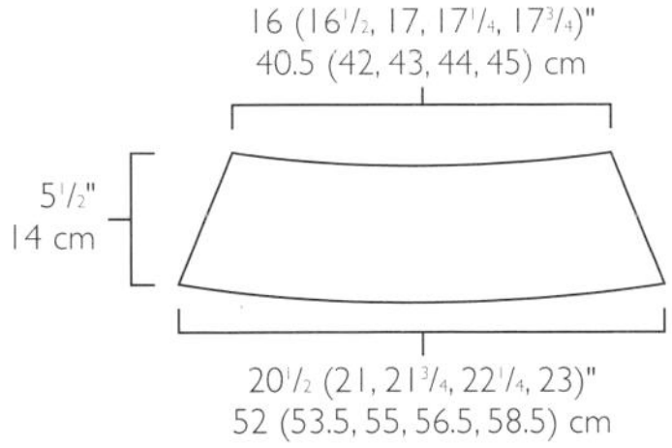
16 (16 1/2, 17, 17 1/4, 17 3/4)"
40.5 (42, 43, 44, 45) cm
5 1/2"
14 cm
20 1/2 (21, 21 3/4, 22 1/4, 23)"
52 (53.5, 55, 56.5, 58.5) cm

Rep Rnds 2 to 5 until 15 rnds total have been worked.

Change to next smaller size hook and continue to rep Rnds 2 to 5 until 22 rnds total have been worked.

Change to smallest size hook and continue to rep Rnds 2 to 5 until 24 rnds total have been worked.

Joining Row: With body inserted inside collar and WS facing, sc tog sts from back to next 51 (53, 55, 58, 61) sts of collar, sc in each of next 21 (21, 21, 20, 19) sts of collar only, sc tog sts from front to next 51 (53, 55, 58, 61) sts of collar, sc in each of next 21 (21, 21, 20, 19) sts of collar only, join with sl st to first sc.

Turn, slip st in each sc around, fasten and end off.

Armhole trims: With RS facing, join to top of armhole, sc evenly down to bottom of armhole, then sc evenly up other side of armhole to collar, fasten and end off. Rep armhole trim across other armhole edge.

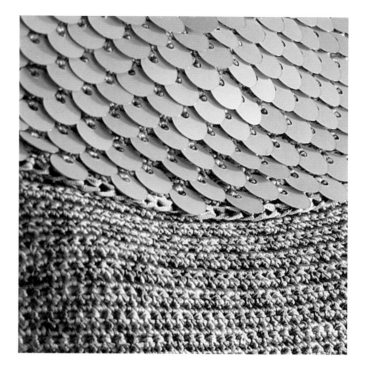

Planning Your Own Patterning and Projects

Luckily, most of the time, beads do not significantly alter a yarn's inherent stitch gauge. Of course, the gauge depends on the motif, how beads are applied, etc. Do I need to remind you that swatching is *always* crucial? This being the case, use any existing pattern for a project as long as you meet gauge, and add your own beadwork to your heart's content. Concentrate on motifs and compositions rather than designing a garment from scratch and figuring out the numbers for yourself. Don't get me wrong—I'm not discouraging you from designing a garment; I just want to show how accessible designing with beads can be. You can incorporate beads on virtually any knit or crochet pattern. Once you start, you might not be able to stop!

The method by which you choose to add beads often depends on the patterning you have in mind. Do you want a bead with a clear direction. Use a heart. Do you want the beads to be prominent? Use the hooked-on or slip-stitch method. Do you want the beads to be integrated into the design? Go for the between-stitches method. Are you using an allover pattern with loads of beads? Prestringing prevents lots of interruptions in the rhythm of your work. Are the motifs you're using isolated, found only in certain spots? Hooking them on is a good solution.

Does your motif have an odd or an even number? Is there an odd or even number of stitches in your project? If you have an odd-numbered motif, such as a heart or diamond, yet your work has an even number of stitches, use the between-stitches method. Do this because an even number of stitches has an odd number of spaces! (Hold up four fingers. Notice that there are three spaces between the four fingers.) Also use the between-stitches method if there is an even number in your motif but an odd number of stitches in your work. (Hold up five fingers. There are four spaces between them.)

If the number in the motif matches that of the work, use any method that places the bead right on the stitch. Try out different methods for the motif (or pattern) to see which yields the best results, looks best to your eye, and that you most enjoy working.

Most cables have an even number. For this reason, I used the between-stitches method of placing the beads in the center of each cable in my Cabled Tunic in Chapter 10. In k1, p1 ribbing, the bead wants to be placed on the protruding knit st, so use the hooked-on method. For crochet, use post-stitches that emulate ribbing; place the bead squarely on the stitch that protrudes (front-post from the right side or back-post from the wrong side). In k2, p2 ribbing, however, the space between the two purls is prime for the between-stitches method. This holds true for two post stitches of crochet.

I've said that beads can either highlight existing stitches or create motifs of their own. Very often, however, they do both! In highlighting the cables of my Cabled Tunic, the beads also create a grid of their own. The beads that sit on the knit stitches or ribbing clearly create their own zigzag lines. In the Crocheted Choker and Necklace in Chapter 16, the beads punctuate the lace edge and the center shells. In the PDA Cover/Purse (see page 96), the beads form their own diamond motifs.

As you're knitting or crocheting, you will find that certain areas just scream for a bead. The center of a diamond, for instance. Or use basic stitches, such as stockinette stitch or single crochet, and let the beads do all the talking, as the saying goes.

To plan bead placement on stitches, make photocopies or scans of the swatch and place some beads on the copy. I find that color copies work best. Substituting flat paper for a knitted swatch makes it easier to handle the beads because they aren't rolling around on a bumpy surface. Go one step further. Scan both beads and stitched fabric and use the cut-and-paste function of any simple graphics program to try different bead arrangements digitally.

To plan bead motifs, gauged graph paper, either physical or virtual, is key. Take a look at any of the stitch charts I offer to get a feel for drawing your own. A special case, however, is the between-stitches method. Since the bead sits between stitches and the box is representative of each stitch across, the bead should actually lie on the line between the boxes, as in the Trompe L'Oeil Cables chart (see page 24).

I've provided blank layouts on pages 133 and 135 of potential bead positions for the between-stitches method (see page 10). Photocopy them to lay out your own designs. The blank layout on page 133 is for knitting and single crochet, and the layout on page 135 is for double crochet.

For knitting and single crochet

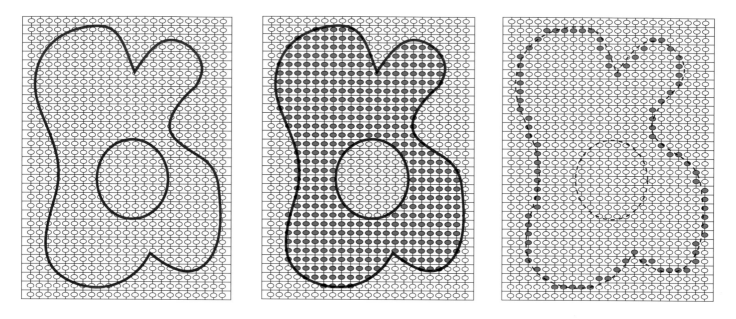

Draw motifs in pencil first.

Fill in the bead spots that fall within the lines of your drawing. An outline is adequate, though you can also fill in the spots.

Determine the size of the motif to learn how many stitches and rows it encompasses. Lastly, draw a purl stitch as a horizontal bar on either side of each bead to ensure that it falls to the right side of the fabric for stitches other than all-reverse-stockinette.

For crochet, this horizontal bar can represent flipped stitches on the right side rows only. There is also a chart for tall crochet stitches, such as double crochet. What the chart does not include, however, are options for lower and higher positions.

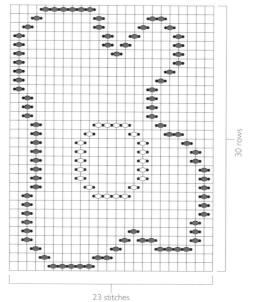

30 rows

23 stitches

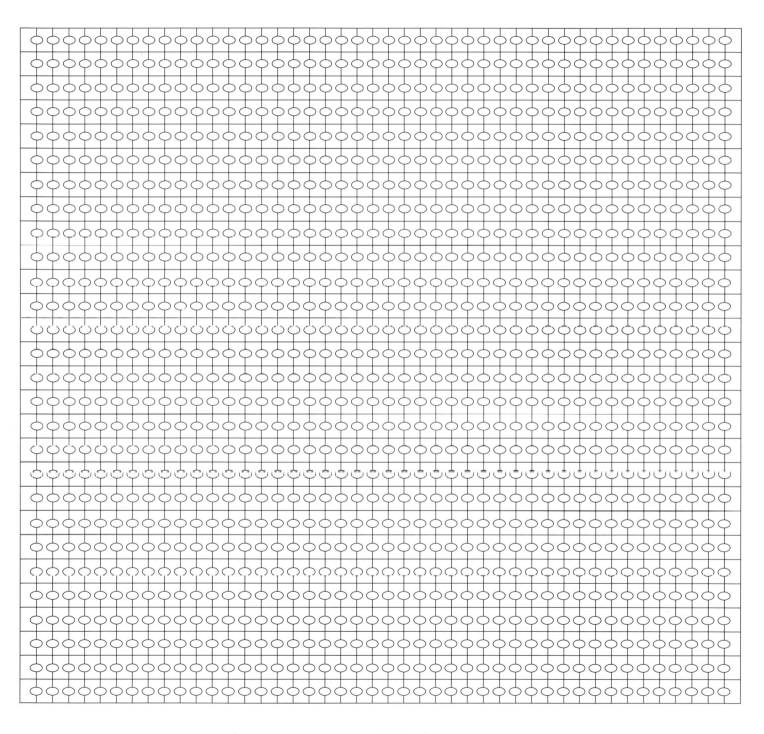

For double crochet

If the first beaded row in the heart motif at below left were a right-side row in knitting, read it as k6, p1, BUB, p1, k6. If it were the first right-side row in single crochet, read it as 5sc, fsc, BUB, fsc, 5sc.

Depending on bead size and tension, creating solid motifs, as opposed to just outlines, may distort patterns and stitches. One option is to place the beads of the motif only on every other stitch/row, which is very much like seed stitch (see heart motif at below right).

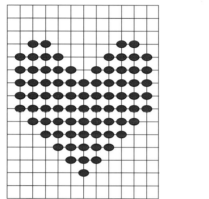
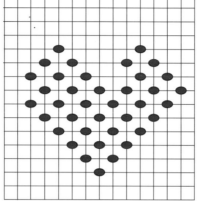

Solid heart vs sparse or scattered heart motifs

If you are "drawing-impaired," fear not. Sticking to simple geometrics can be very effective; so is using letters of the alphabet.

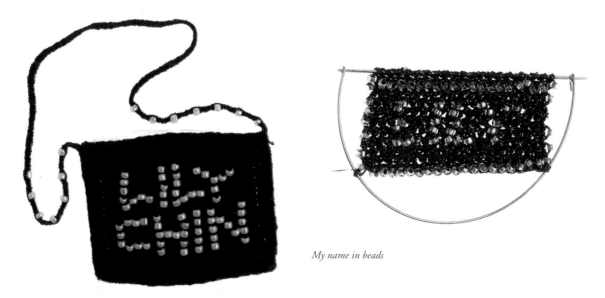

My name in beads

Computers make designing easy. Graphics programs offer simple drawing tools. Complex programs allow you to create a layer (very much like tracing paper) and follow the lines of an existing image. After drawing over the image, delete the image and keep the tracing. Lay the tracing over the beaded grid.

Another way of quickly previewing what the beadwork looks like is to sew beads on the swatch. An even faster approach is to sew beads on paper. Paper is ideal for the slipped-stitch method of Chapter 3 or the separate-strand method of Chapter 7. Use gauged graph paper. Try to get one that perfectly matches your stitch gauge; you can see the actual size of your stitches. Thread a tapestry needle and puncture the paper on the vertical lines to represent the strand of yarn coming in or out between stitches. Working from vertical line to vertical line, place beads on the yarn before inserting the needle through the paper again. *Note:* This method is not dissimilar to those yarn-sewing cards for kids!

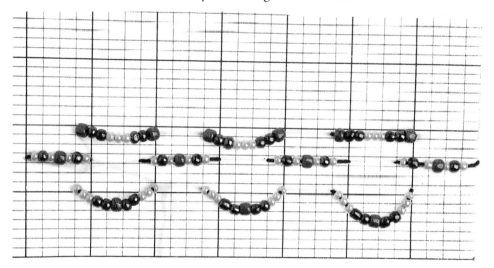

Piercing gauged graph paper with thread, needle, and beads

If you're still at a loss about incorporating beads into your work, take inspiration from Rorschach tests. Used by psychiatrists, these ink-blot tests are indicative of how you view things. What do the beads look like? What do they remind you of? Do scattered black beads make you think of watermelon seeds? Design an intarsia motif of a watermelon, then, with the beads as seeds (use seed beads, as a matter of fact!). Some beads might look like strawberry seeds, in which case work up a strawberry motif and add beads. Silver beads remind me of stars in a night sky. That's how my Moon-Face Beret was born.

Free associate. Think of things that feature bumpy or shiny textures. Some of my fantasy items are spawned from exactly this line of thinking. Thinking of shiny things led me to snakes which in turn led to my crocheting "Cleopatra's Asp," using red beads for eyes and gold beads in a circular cording stitch (the beads wind up spiraling around). You'll find this same type of coiled cording in my PDA Cover/Purse (see page 96). Other than this advice, you will not find directions for the costumes depicted here. They are meant only to inspire you.

To complete Cleopatra's outfit, the beaded collar features colors found on King Tut's tomb. The collar features side-to-side construction and short-row shaping.

Moon-face beret

Cleopatra's asp

Cleopatra's collar

My stint as the Little Mermaid had me hunting for shell beads. Worked in watery and shimmery hues reminiscent of a tropical ocean, the shawl boasts actual sea shells around the edges. They are crocheted in using the hooked method.

I've furthered this theme by knitting a clamshell bra with ridged ribbing lines. Pearl beads are tambour-embroidered into the recesses of the purl lines.

Little Mermaid shell shawl

Little Mermaid shell bra

Lastly, the fishtail skirt of the mermaid's dress uses blue and green spangles to duplicate the look of fish scales. I crocheted the freshwater pearl trim at the neck and sleeves with the separate-strands method.

Little Mermaid dress

At the Stitches show, a national knitting conference where I teach (held in three locations throughout the year), it's now expected that I dress up for banquet night in some outrageous ensemble. Indeed, HGTV's television program, *Sew Much More,* has done a segment on my costumes throughout the years. These knitted and/or crocheted outfits included the Cleopatra pieces shown here, as well as the Little Mermaid. I've also dressed up as Wonder Woman, Scarlett O'Hara, Pebbles Flintstone, and others (but beads were not a part of these ensembles).

If neither images nor pictures nor fantasy items excite you, think in terms of trim only. Not only does beaded trim conserve on beads, it adds just enough subtle accent to highlight an otherwise ho-hum item. To "etch" the outlines of your projects, use the beaded long-tailed cast-on innovation from the Ethereal Lace Tunic in Chapter 6, or end with the beaded bind-off from the Patagonian Night Sky Scarf of Chapter 2. You can add beads from the end. Reel off 7 times the width of the bind-off row, clip yarn, then string beads from the end. You can actually pick up stitches, then bind off with beads for trims around curves and edges in the same manner. In crochet, just work beaded single crochet around pieces.

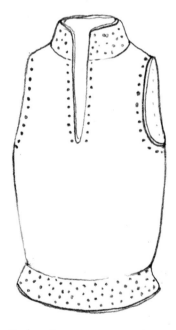

Beads as trim on garment

Belts, jewelry, scarves, and other accessories are great small projects for trying out ideas without a whole lot of investment in time or money. Think, too, about how to make things reversible! Since items such as belts and scarves flip around, beads should be as prominent on one side as they are on the other.

Color and texture are some of the easiest things in a design to change and vary. Don't just stick to my hues. Indeed, I encourage individual variation. Instead of a matte bead, try a shiny one. In lieu of charcoal and gray, try burgundy and pink. A different shade of bead and/or yarn has the ability to change the very feel and mood of a piece, transforming it from classy to funky, from subdued to sizzling.

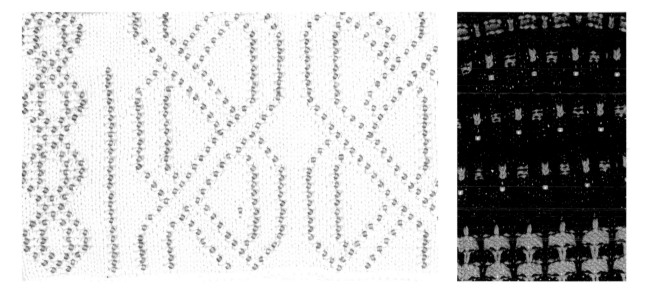

Various color alternatives

One idea I haven't addressed is the use of variegated yarns. There are even variegated beads, too! Be careful when using these multihued yarns, however. Often, if a bead is not a strong enough contrast, it can get lost among the profusion of colors. View my swatches to see what works and what doesn't. You decide. Even with a project, there's plenty of opportunity for personalization. Try different colored yarns in each section. Try different colored beads in each section. Or keep the same yarn color throughout and vary the beads. What about using different colors of beads for every stripe? As you can tell, the choices go on and on. . . .

Just because you may do one craft (i.e., knit vs crochet) does not mean you cannot draw inspiration from the other. Indeed, it is very possible to match knit gauges to single crochet, for instance. Thus, projects such as the Shimmy Camisole or the PDA Cover/Purse may be knitted instead of crocheted. Conversely, projects like the knitted Ethereal Lace Tunic, the Cabled Tunic, and the Vargas Girl Pullover are accessible to crocheters. Expand your horizons—but remember to always swatch first!

Variegated yarns with variegated beads (lower left yarn is solid)

Conclusion

I have a yarn stash that rivals Imelda Marcos' shoe collection. It is a veritable warehouse of yarn that weighs over a ton . . . literally. That's more than 2,000 pounds! Never wanting to surrender even the most mundane of strands, I find that beads invigorate the stash. Yarn that used to look a bit old or drab or dull can be revitalized with the addition of beads. A yarn that was bought on sale, yet was in a less-than-ideal color, takes on new life as I mix it with a color of bead that gives it a new cast. "Plain vanilla" yarns are no longer that. Instead, they are potential bead carriers. Even novelty yarns can be jazzed up with the addition of beads.

All of a sudden, a fresh and new world of color, texture, and possibility takes over. My stash is looking better and better. Armed with all these techniques and applications, yours should, too. Soon you may find yourself building up a bead stash as well. I have. And luckily, beads do not take up as much space as yarns!

Abbreviations

B1	applied bead added to flipped single crochet	dc	double crochet	sk2p	slip 1, k2tog, pass slipped stitch over
bch	beaded chain	dec(s)	decrease(s)	sl	slip
bdc	beaded double crochet	dpn(s)	double-pointed needle(s)	sl st	slip stitch
beg	begin(ning)	fdcdb	flipped double crochet with double beads	ssc	spangled single crochet
bfsc	beaded flipped single crochet	foll	following	ssk	slip 2 sts one at time as if to knit, return both sts to left needle and knit them tog through their back loops
bhdc	beaded half-double crochet	hdc	half-double crochet		
		inc(s)	increase(s)		
BK1	bead knit 1	lp(s)	loop(s)		
BO	bind off	k	knit		
BP1	bcad purl 1	k2tog	knit 2 together	sp(s)	space(s)
bsc	beaded single crochet	m	marker	st(s)	stitch(es)
BSTB	beaded strand to back: bring beaded strand to back of work and resume working with both strands tog	M1	make 1 increase: with the left needle tip, lift the strand between the needles from front to back and knit the lifted strand through the back loop to increase 1	St st	stockinette stitch
				tbl	through back loop
				tog	together
				trc	treble crochet
				W&T	wrap and turn: with yarn in back, slip the next st to right needle as if to purl, bring yarn to front between the needles, return slipped st to the left needle, turn work
BSTF	beaded strand to front: separate both strands and bring beaded strand to front of work	meas	measure(s)		
		ndl(s)	needle(s)		
		p	purl		
BUB	bring up bead close to needle or hook	patt(s)	pattern(s)	WS	wrong side
		pm	place marker	wyib	with yarn in back
BUBL	bring up long bead	psso	pass slipped st(s) over	wyif	with yarn in front
BUBR	bring up round bead	rem(s)	remain(s)	yo	yarnover
ch(s)	chain(s)	rep(s)	repeat(s)	yon	yarn around needle producing a knitwise yo
cont	continue	rnd(s)	round(s)		
CO	cast on	RS	right side		
dbdc	double bead double crochet	sc	single crochet		
		sk	skip		

Suppliers

Materials featured in this book have been supplied by:

Anny Blatt USA, Inc., 7796 Boardwalk, Brighton, MI 48116; (248) 486-6160; (800) 531-9276; info@annyblattusa.com.

Aurora Yarns, PO Box 3068, Moss Beach, CA 94038; (650) 728-2730; aurorayarns@pacbell.net.

Beads World, Inc., 1384 Broadway, New York, NY 10018; (212) 302-1199; www.beadsworldusa.com; beadsworld@aol.com.

Brown Sheep Company, 100662 County Road 16, Mitchell, NE 69357; (800) 826-9136; www.brownsheep.com.

Bryson Distributing, 4065 W. 11th Ave. #39, Eugene, OR 97402; (800) 544-8992; www.brysonknits.com.

Classic Elite Yarns, 300 Jackson St., Lowell, MA 01852; (800) 343-0308; knit@classicelite.com; www.classiceliteyarns.com.

Crystal Palace Yarns, 2320 Bissell Ave., Richmond, CA 94804; (510) 237-9988; (800) 666-7455; www.straw.com.

Fire Mountain Gems and Beads, One Fire Mountain Way, Grants Pass, OR 97526-2373; (800) 423-2319; www.firemountaingems.com.

Gay Bowles Sales—Mill Hill, PO Box 1060, Janesville, WI 53547-1060; (608) 754-9466; www.millhillbeads.com; millhill@millhill.com.

Karabella Yarns, 1201 Broadway, New York, NY 10001; (212) 684-2665; www.karabellayarns.com.

Kruh Knits, 1570 Howard Gap Rd., Tryon, NC 28782; (800) 248-KNIT (5648).

Lion Brand Yarn, 34 West 15th St., New York, NY 10011; (800) 258-YARN (9276); www.lionbrand.com.

Louet Sales, 808 Commerce Park Dr., Ogdensburg, NY 13669; (613) 925-4502; (800) 897-6444; info@louet.com; www.louet.com.

Sandaga, div. of Bhens Products, 1231 Broadway, New York, NY 10001, (212) 532-6820.

Shipwreck Beads, 8560 Commerce Place Dr. NE, Lacey, WA 98516; (360) 754-2323; (800) 950-4232; www.shipwreckbeads.com.

Skacel Collection, Inc., PO Box 88110, Seattle, WA 98138-2110; 253-854-2710; www.skacelknitting.com.

Threads, Sutter Place Mall, 5221 South 48th St., Lincoln, NE 68516; (402) 489-9550; www.threads-ne.com.

Toho Shoji (New York), Inc., 990 Sixth Ave., New York, NY 10018; (212) 868-7465 or 7466; tohoshoj@webjapan.com.

Westminster Fibers, Inc., 4 Townsend West, Unit 8, Nashua, NH 03063; (603) 886-5041; wfibers@aol.com.

Sources and Further Reading

Brown, Nancy. *The Crocheter's Companion.* Loveland, Colorado: Interweave Press, 2002.

Chin, Lily. "Designing for the Machine: Color & Texture—Beads," *Machine Knit America,* May/June 1994, Vol. 3, No. 6, 9–12, 47–49.

————. "Draw a Bead on Knits," *Knitter's,* Summer 1995, No. 39, 63–65.

————. "Garden of Beadin'," *Knitter's,* Summer 1995, No. 39, 58–63.

————. "Neo-Norwegian Beaded Tunic, Rethinking the Classic Norwegian," *Knitter's,* Fall 1993, No. 32, 34–39.

Durant, Judith, and Jean Campbell. *The Beader's Companion.* Loveland, Colorado: Interweave Press, 1998.

Timmons, Christine. "Hand-Knitting Techniques," from *Threads* Magazine." Newtown, Connecticut: The Taunton Press, 1991.

Kooler, Donna. *Donna Kooler's Encyclopedia of Crochet.* Little Rock, Arkansas: Leisure Arts, 2002.

Korach, Alice. "Bead Knitting Madness," *Threads,* August/September 1989, No. 24, 24–29.

Square, Vicki. *The Knitter's Companion.* Loveland, Colorado: Interweave Press, 1996.

Thomas, Mary. *Mary Thomas' Knitting Book.* London: Hodder and Stoughton, Ltd., 1938. Reprint: New York: Dover Publications, 1972.

Vogue Knitting. *Vogue Knitting: The Ultimate Knitting Book.* New York: Pantheon Books, 1989.

Index

Page numbers in boldface refer to illustrations.